Animals
like us

DK

Animals
like us

In association with

ARKive

LONDON, NEW YORK,
MELBOURNE, MUNICH, AND DELHI

Written and edited by Andrea Mills
Art Editor Joanne Little
Senior Editor Fran Jones
Senior Art Editor Joanne Connor
Managing Editor Linda Esposito
Managing Art Editor Jane Thomas
Art Director Simon Webb
Publishing Director Jonathan Metcalf
Production Controller Alison Lenane
Picture Researcher Sarah Pownall
DK Picture Library Sarah Mills
DTP Designer Natasha Lu
Consultant Kim Bryan
ARKive Director Richard Edwards

First American Edition, 2005
Published in the United States by
DK Publishing, Inc., 375 Hudson Street,
New York, New York 10014

05 06 07 08 09   10 9 8 7 6 5 4 3 2 1

A Cataloging-in-Publication record for this book
is available from the Library of Congress.

ISBN 0-7566-1008-7

Color reproduction by Colourscan, Singapore
Printed and bound in China by Leo Paper Group

Discover more at
www.dk.com

Forest

Desert

Ocean

Grassland

Mountain

Contents

6   A message from Sir David Attenborough

8   Forest
10   Orangutan
12   Kakapo
14   Verreaux's sifaka

16   Koala
18   Tiger
20   Forest watch

22   Desert
24   African elephant
26   Wild Bactrian camel
28   Arabian oryx

30   Gila monster
32   Indian wild ass
34   Desert watch

36   Ocean
38   Humpback whale
40   Sea otter
42   Marine iguana

44   West Indian manatee
46   Green turtle
48   Ocean watch

50   Grassland
52   Cheetah
54   Black rhinoceros
56   Hyacinth macaw

58   Grevy's zebra
60   Giant anteater
62   Grassland watch

64   Mountain
66   Giant panda
68   Ethiopian wolf
70   Mountain gorilla

72   Snow leopard
74   Spectacled bear
76   Mountain watch

78   How you can help
80   Index and Credits

A message from ARKive's patron, Sir David Attenborough

We live on a very special planet, one we are lucky to share with many millions of amazing animals. Like us, animals have made their homes all over the world—in forests, deserts, oceans, grasslands, and mountains. These places are known as "habitats" and each one provides the animals that live there with everything they need—food, water, shelter, and the chance to meet a mate.

Although the world is a big place, it is becoming very crowded. There are more people than ever before and they too all need food, water, and somewhere to live. The world's habitats are being changed or destroyed as more and more people make their homes in these wild places. Animals are finding it harder to survive. They are being crowded out, driven from their homes, captured for trade, and killed for food or sport. As a result, many are now seriously threatened with extinction. This means they may soon disappear completely and forever, unless we do something to save them.

The more we know about these animals, the more we can do to help them. ARKive is collecting films and photographs of the world's threatened animals in a giant digital library and building a huge wildlife Web site, so that everyone can learn more about these animals and the urgent need to protect them and their habitats.

Featuring some of the threatened animals found in ARKive, this book shows us what these animals look like, what their lives are really like, the problems they face, and what is special about each and every one of them. I hope that you too will get involved and help make sure these amazing animals continue to share our planet, before it is too late.

Sir David Attenborough CH FRS

ARKive
www.arkive.org

Orangutan

Kakapo

Forest

In the forests, there are more plants and animals than in any other habitat on land. Forests are areas of land with dense tree cover, and there are three main types. Rainforests are wet and warm with the greatest variety of animals. Temperate forests are cooler, with trees that shed their leaves. Coniferous forests are colder, with fewer animals.

Forest facts

● **Paper is made** from the pulp of many different types of trees.

● **At least half** a million types of animals live in forests.

● **The Amazon** in South America is the world's largest rainforest. It covers more than a third of Brazil.

● **Half of the world's** forests have been chopped down.

Verreaux's sifaka

Koala

Tiger

Threats to forests

When trees are cut down and forests destroyed, it is known as deforestation. The wood is used to make paper and furniture. The land is cleared to make room for farms, houses, and roads. People often light fires to clear the land, and this leaves animals homeless.

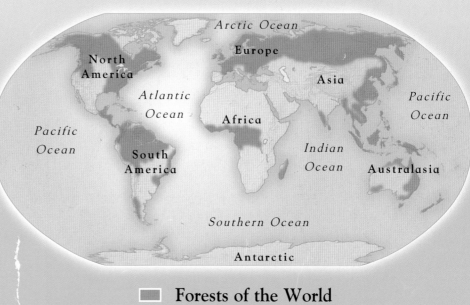

Arctic Ocean

Europe

North America

Asia

Atlantic Ocean

Pacific Ocean

Africa

Pacific Ocean

South America

Indian Ocean

Australasia

Southern Ocean

Antarctic

Forests of the World

Orangutan

I'm a lot like you. Look how I grip things with my hands. I can also walk like you, but my feet are more useful than yours. They work like an extra pair of hands. We have other things in common too, like a sweet tooth, flexible joints, and the fact that we catch the same diseases. I even sleep in a bed, but I build a new one every night!

We try to escape the sun.
When the sun is beating down, we drape large leaves over our heads—they're perfect sun hats! Branches are useful, too. We use them as tools to dig out honey from the nests of bees or poke for ants and bugs in tree holes.

We catch raindrops in our mouths.
The rain's great if we feel thirsty. We just open our mouths wide and let the drops fall in! If the rain gets too heavy, we can always make umbrellas out of leaves. In the forest, they're never hard to find.

Did you know?

Our name means "people of the forest" in Malay.

We are the largest tree-living animals in the world.

We are the only nonhuman great apes to live outside Africa.

The relationship between mother and baby orangutans is said to be the strongest bond in the animal kingdom.

We can live for up to 45 years.

I live with my mom.
My dad didn't stay around to see me born, so Mom raised me on her own. I clung to Mom's tummy until I was one. I'll stay with her until I'm about eight.

Fruit is my favorite food.
There are hundreds of fruits in the rainforest. When I'm older, I'll be able to remember where to find ripe fruit. I also eat flowers, insects, bark, and seeds.

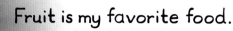

Fact file

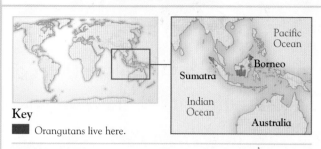

Key
▉ Orangutans live here.

Population

🐵 = 5,000

The number is estimated at fewer than 20,000.

1990	🐵🐵🐵🐵🐵🐵🐵🐵🐵🐵 50,000
2003	🐵🐵🐵🐵 fewer than 20,000

Orangutans under threat

Deforestation People are cutting down forests at a rapid rate. Since 1980, as much as 80 percent of orangutan habitat has vanished.

Forest fires In 1997, fires in Borneo destroyed much of the forest—a third of the orangutan population died.

Pet trade Orangutans have been illegally transported in the pet trade. However, because of stricter laws, this is now less of a threat.

The view is great up here!
The rainforest is my home, and the trees are my playground. My fingers and toes grab the branches tightly when I'm swinging. I'd beat you at arm-wrestling because my arms are strong and longer than my whole body.

96 percent of orangutan genes are the same as human genes. Their hands are like human hands with a thumb and four fingers.

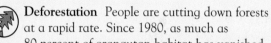

My cheeks will grow huge!
When I grow up, I'll look like this guy with big, padded cheeks. My mom says they're very attractive. She also told me to avoid other males when I become an adult or I could end up getting in trouble. These guys chase and fight a lot.

Kakapo

I'm a record-breaker! Not only am I the longest-living bird in the world, but I'm the heaviest parrot, too. You'll know when I'm nearby—that scent of honey and flowers is actually my natural odor. Unfortunately, I smell so strong that dogs and cats can easily find me. For my own protection, I've been moved from the New Zealand mainland to two of its tiny islands.

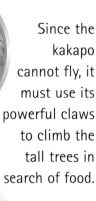

Since the kakapo cannot fly, it must use its powerful claws to climb the tall trees in search of food.

Did you know?

Early settlers to New Zealand kept kakapos as pets.

Experts think that thousands of years ago we were lighter and able to fly. Over time, we've put on weight and stopped flying.

Some kakapos are estimated to have lived for more than 60 years.

Male kakapos make a low booming noise to attract the ladies. A kakapo can make thousands of booms in just one night.

I'm the only parrot who can't fly.

That's why I hop around the forest. I have big thighs under my feathers, which are ideal for long-distance walking to find food. My wings are virtually useless, although they do help me to balance if I'm up in a tree.

Look at our picture-postcard new home!

We now live on two tiny islands called Chalky and Codfish. Life's a long vacation here. There are no predators, and the food is fantastic. We hope there will soon be more of us, thanks to this safe haven.

 To learn more about kakapos, visit the Kakapo Recovery Program at www.kakaporecovery.org.nz

We're known as "the parrots of the night".
That's because we go exploring and looking for food when it's dark. Mothers raise their families without any help, so they must find food for their offspring. This means babies are left unprotected while their mothers go out. The forest was a dark, scary place without my mom.

Our enemies include rats like this one.
When people arrived in New Zealand, they brought dogs, cats, and rats. These animals caught us easily. Now, we've been moved away from them for our own safety.

I'm strictly vegetarian.
Almonds, apples, and walnuts are my favorites. The leaves, seeds, and stems of some plants are also tasty. It's worth the effort of climbing a tree when you get to the top and discover that the fruit is ripe and juicy.

When I sense danger, I freeze on the spot.
As I ramble through the bushes at night, I make sure I keep my wits about me. If I'm disturbed by a strange noise or an unusual smell, I stay completely still. I hold the same position and try to blend in with the greenery because I can't fly away to escape.

Fact file

Key
■ Kakapos live here.

Population

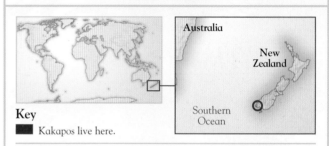

= 25

It is hoped that the kakapo population will grow now that they have been moved to two safe islands.

1977 | 167
2004 | 83

Kakapos under threat

⊕ **Hunting** In the past, the kakapo was hunted for its feathers and meat. Hunters found this flightless bird an easy target.

🐾 **Breeding problems** Kakapos reproduce when certain trees have ripe fruit to eat. This means the kakapo does not nest every year.

or listen to the male kakapo making his booming call to attract the females at www.arkive.org/kakapo

Verreaux's sifaka

"Shifak!" If you hear me make this noise, beware. It's my alarm call. My name comes from the shriek I give to warn other sifakas in my group of danger. If we end up in a confrontation with another group of sifakas, there's no fighting—we just growl and leap around. But up in the tall trees of Madagascar, we usually lead a quiet life.

Babies must hold tight!
We cling to our mothers soon after we're born. Mom jumped around looking for food with me attached. I grasped her tummy for the first month, then she carried me on her back.

Did you know?

We live on the world's fourth-largest island, just east of Africa.

Madagascar is home to a variety of creatures found nowhere else in the world. This includes 200 types of birds, 300 types of reptiles, and 175 types of frogs.

We belong to the group of primates known as lemurs.

We must look out for attacks from the air. Birds such as the Madagascar harrier-hawk swoop down to catch us.

My activities change with the seasons.
I sleep in during the dry season because the mornings arc too cold to look for food. I go out later when the day warms up. But in the wet season, I only go out before sunrise and after sunset. The rest of the day is far too hot!

This is my home and my dinner.
Not only do I live in these trees, but they taste good, too. During the dry season, I eat leaves. There are heavy morning dews at this time, and I lick the water from my fur. When it's the rainy season, I eat fruit and flowers. I sometimes eat soil, too—it sounds horrible to you, but it seems to help my digestion.

I love tree-jumping.
To get from one tree to the next, we cling to a stump or branch, then push off and take a flying leap. My long fingers and toes give me a firm grip. Since my eyes face forward like yours do, I'm good at judging distances. In one single jump I've been known to leap an impressive 33 ft (10 m).

Learn about the sifaka by visiting Primate of the Week at www.staff.washington.edu/timk/primate

Fact file

Key

▇ Verreaux's sifakas live here.

Africa

Indian Ocean

Population

👤 = 20,000

There are no current population figures available, but a 1992 estimate suggested there were more than 100,000 Verreaux's sifakas.

1992 | 👤 👤 👤 👤 👤   more than 100,000

Verreaux's sifakas under threat

Deforestation Trees are being cut down and used as firewood, so sifakas lose their homes.

Hunting Madagascan hunters find sifakas an easy target because of the open bushland.

Forest fires There is evidence of people deliberately starting fires in parts of the region.

What a mover!

Our skipping, hopping, and jumping makes it look as though we're dancing. If you see us bounding along on the ground, it's usually because we're crossing open spaces where there are no trees for us to leap between. We often spread our arms out for balance.

It's unusual to see me sunbathing on the ground.

Most of the time, I sunbathe high up in the treetops with the other sifakas. If I do come down from the trees to sunbathe, you'll get the best view of me. I sit down, make myself comfortable, and stretch out my arms to soak up the sun.

The legs of a sifaka are longer and more powerful than the arms. This is why a sifaka is so good at jumping. The strength in the legs propels them from tree to tree.

Koala

How do I get up here?

Well, it isn't easy. I break into a run, spring off the ground, then dig my claws into the tree. Once I'm steady, I climb higher up the branch. Look for claw marks where I've gripped the bark. Near the top, I make myself comfortable. My super-furry bottom makes a perfect cushion on the rough branches.

Believe me, two thumbs are better than one.

I've got two thumbs on each front paw. These help me climb trees, clutch bark, and hold food more easily. I'm active at night, so I sleep in the treetops most of the day. We return to the same trees and think of them as home.

Many people think that a koala is a bear. In fact, it is a marsupial. This means the mother carries her baby in a pouch on her tummy.

Did you know?

Our fur differs according to where we live in Australia. It is thicker in the south where winters are colder.

Males have a scent gland in the middle of their chests, which they rub on trees to mark out territory.

Baby koalas eat special Mom-droppings called pap. Pap contains the bacteria we need to break down the tough eucalyptus leaves.

Our back paws have two toes joined together. We use this as a grooming claw and bug remover.

Here's a baby koala hitching a ride.

A baby is called a "joey." Like all joeys, I was the same size as a jelly bean when I was born. For the first seven months, I lived inside Mom's pouch. As I got heavier, she put me on her back.

Help protect the koala by visiting the Australian Koala Foundation at www.savethekoala.com

Fact file

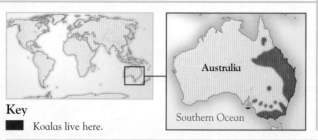

Key

■ Koalas live here.

Australia

Southern Ocean

Population

 =20,000

2004 | 🐨🐨🐨🐨🐨 100,000

No one can agree on the exact number of koalas. Although one current estimate is 100,000 koalas, not all experts go along with this number.

Koalas under threat

Deforestation When forests are cut down, koalas have to eat more leaves from the trees that remain. These trees cannot replace their leaves quickly enough and they die. Koalas then starve.

Increased human population People have moved into koala habitats, bringing with them domestic dogs and cars. Every year, about 4,000 koalas are killed by dog attacks or car accidents.

I'm going to be here for a while.
All of us spend most of the night eating. We are picky eaters—we only eat the freshest leaves of a few types of gum trees. Other animals find the leaves poisonous, so that means more leaves for us!

There is a scientific reason I'm this lazy.
It's essential that I sleep a lot because my diet of leaves doesn't provide me with much energy. I sleep for up to 18 hours a day. In fact, I was asleep before you disturbed me, so if you don't mind… zzzz.

Did I just hear this branch creak?
Trees have to be strong when we all get together! As soon as one of us has sniffed out some fresh leaves, the others come to get a taste. If you hear groups of us making noises like snoring and burping, please don't think we're being rude. This is our way of talking to each other, and the sounds make sense to us.

or watch koalas enjoying a feast high in the gum trees at www.arkive.org/koala ✉ 17

Tiger

Come closer. Don't be scared. Although we're the biggest cats in the world, we only bite when we're really hungry! You're lucky—I've already eaten today. Apart from people who hunt us and other tigers, I have little to fear. Most of the forest creatures are terrified of my strong jaws, sharp teeth, and huge roar.

I was a lucky cub. Only about half of all cubs born survive to become adults. Like all cubs, I was born blind and helpless. My eyes opened after a week. I was fully independent within two years.

A reflecting layer at the back of a tiger's eye mirrors the light so that it has much better vision in the dark.

I'm the only tiger with these stripes. No two tigers have the same pattern of stripes. In the same way, no two people have the same set of fingerprints. My stripes blend in with the trees, so I can move around unseen.

Did you know?

I'm a Bengal tiger, living in India. There are also four other types of tigers found in Asia. These are the Amoy, Indo-Chinese, Sumatran, and Siberian tigers.

The heaviest tiger in the wild was a male Siberian. He weighed the same as four adult men.

Tigers and lions are the largest mammals on land to eat only meat.

We can live for up to 15 years in the wild.

Read stories and legends about the tiger by visiting Project Tiger at www.projecttiger.nic.in

I make quite a splash!

I've heard that other cats are scared of going in rivers and streams, but tigers love swimming. It's the only way to cool off in this constant heat. I'm not one to boast, but I do consider myself to be an excellent swimmer. Next time the sun's out, I'll be looking for somewhere to paddle my paws.

Mom taught me everything I know.

When I was a few months old, I began wandering around the forest with Mom. She showed me how to hunt and kill. I learned the importance of having a territory. Within this area, I can find enough food and won't run into too many rivals.

Be very afraid at sunset.

That's when I go out hunting alone. I can cover 20 miles (32 km) in one night. All I eat is meat, so finding my dinner requires time and patience. About one out of every 15 hunts results in a meal, which is often a deer or a wild pig.

I defend my territory.

Once I'd chosen the territory I wanted, I made it my own. Scent and scratch marks let other tigers know it's mine. It's not easy to protect these areas. I've known tigers who died in fights over boundaries.

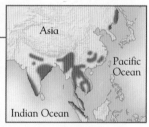

Fact file

Asia

Pacific Ocean

Indian Ocean

Key

■ All species of tigers live here.

Population

 = 10,000

In 1900, there were about 100,000 tigers. Today, fewer than 7,000 tigers remain.

| 1900 | | 100,000 |
| 2004 | fewer than 7,000 | |

Tigers under threat

⊕ **Hunting** They are illegally hunted for their fur. Also, tiger parts are used in traditional medicine.

🏠 **Habitat loss** Land is being used to feed and house the rapidly growing Asian population.

🐾 **Lack of food** The food source of tigers is greatly reduced due to increased hunting.

Forest watch

From the Philippine eagle soaring across the sky to the golden frog who lays its eggs on the damp forest floor, all kinds of animals have made the forests their home. Many are vegetarians, such as the pygmy hippo, who makes the most of the supply of leaves, roots, and fruit. Others are hungry meat-eaters, such as the wolverine, who roams the forest stalking unsuspecting prey.

Philippine eagle
I'm one of the world's largest eagles, standing almost 3 ft (1 m) tall. My nickname is the monkey-eating eagle because I've been known to swoop down and snatch monkeys from the trees. I tear them with my talons. That is why I have such a ferocious reputation in the Philippine Islands where I live.

 Forests have been cleared to build houses and make farmland.

 People set traps to catch wolverines. Their fur is used to make clothing.

Wolverine
Watch out! I eat any animal I find—I'd eat you if I could. My jaws can bite through frozen meat and bones. Here in the icy North American forests, even the wolves are afraid of my strength and leave their prey when I arrive.

Golden frog
Don't touch me—my skin is toxic. Its bright color warns predators to stay away. At home in Madagascar, I look for insects in sunny spots. I love to snack on a fruit fly or a juicy ant. If you hear a frog chorus, it's us males singing to attract female frogs.

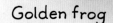

 These frogs are very popular in the pet trade. People have collected too many.

Mandrill

You can't miss me! I'm the largest monkey in the world—and the most colorful mammal, too. In the African rainforests, I stand out because of my red nose, blue cheeks, yellow beard, and bright blue bottom. We live in big, noisy groups. By day, we search for food on the ground, and at night we sleep up in the trees.

 Many trees in the pygmy hippo's habitat are being cleared.

Pygmy hippo

I'm a small hippopotamus who lives in the forest. Our name comes from the Greek words for "river horse." This isn't a bad description of us. By day we wallow in the swamps and rivers of western Africa or rest in the hollows of the river banks. After dark, we head for dry land to munch on the delicious plants. Our hearing and eyesight are excellent so we can stay alert to danger.

 People have hunted mandrills by setting traps for them. Mandrill meat is eaten in some places.

Asiatic lion

I'm the king of the beasts. With my striking mane, powerful body, and deadly jaws, most people around the world consider me the animal king. In the Gir Forest of western India where I live, you'll hear my loud roar throughout the night as I assert my authority. But if it goes quiet, I'm probably just devouring my latest meaty catch. Hmmm—my mouth is watering at the thought!

 These kings of the jungle are highly prized by hunters. They are regarded as top hunting trophies.

21

African elephant

Wild Bactrian camel

Desert

If the rainfall in an area is less than 10 in (25 cm) a year, then the land is called a desert. A typical desert is very dry with extreme temperatures. Days are hot and nights are cold. The landscape consists of sand or rock. Few animals can survive here, and many are only active at night when it is cooler. Some have to get the water they need from their food.

Desert facts

- The Gobi in Asia is hot in summer, with temperatures below freezing in winter.

- The biggest desert in the world is the Sahara in Africa.

- The Atacama in South America is the driest desert. No rain falls here. The only moisture in the area is from fog!

- The tallest sand dune is found in the Sahara. It is about three times taller than the Great Pyramid in Egypt.

Arabian oryx

Gila monster

Indian wild ass

Threats to deserts

An increase in human population and better technology means that people can use the desert to grow food and graze their animals. As a result, there are fewer desert plants. Many animals can't survive without these plants because they are their main source of food and water.

Arctic Ocean

North America

Europe

Asia

Atlantic Ocean

Pacific Ocean

Pacific Ocean

Africa

South America

Indian Ocean

Australasia

Southern Ocean

Antarctic

☐ Deserts of the World

African elephant

It's no wonder my nickname is Jumbo—look at me! I weigh the same as four cars, and that makes me the heaviest animal on land. I live in Africa, and my ears are almost the same shape as a map of this continent. We have few enemies in the desert because the other animals are too small to challenge us. Well, would you be brave enough?

For two whole years, my tusks were not visible. Then they started to pop out. Like all baby elephants, I stayed close to my mom for about five years. She was patient, even when I made a mess while learning to pour water into my mouth!

Spiky plants are no problem to eat. My big teeth grind up tough vegetation thoroughly. Although I only eat grass, leaves, bark, and fruit, I'm chewing away for about 18 hours every day.

Did you know?

I live in the desert, but other African elephants live in grasslands and forests.

Lions and crocodiles may attack and kill baby elephants.

See my tusks? These are ivory teeth, and they never stop growing.

Male elephants are called bulls and females are called cows.

As you are left- or right-handed, we are left- or right-tusked. We use one tusk much more than the other.

Where would I be without my trunk? I don't like to think about it. Every day my trunk helps me perform so many tasks. At various times, it's a nose, a hand, another foot, a digger, a duster, and a way of signaling. More often than not, though, I use it for getting food, as you can see!

See the African elephant by visiting the African Wildlife Foundation at www.awf.org/wildlives

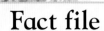

Fact file

Africa

Atlantic
Ocean

Key
 African elephants live here.

Population

 = 200,000

Hunting is the main reason for the
dramatic fall in African elephant numbers.

1980	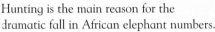	1,340,000
2004		fewer than 660,000

African elephants under threat

 Hunting African elephants have been hunted
for their ivory tusks for a long time. The fact
that elephants are so large makes them an easy
target for hunters.

 Increased human population As people
move in, the elephant habitat is reduced. Elephants
then have less space in which to find their food.

Watch out for our elephant processions!

You wouldn't want to get trampled on by these feet. We travel
in lines to find water and food. We sometimes make a
long journey through the desert to get to a water hole.

We wrestle with our trunks.

It's usually males who fight
like this. Most of the time
we live in friendly groups
where we greet and touch
each other. Being part of
a group is important to us.
If any family member is sick or
hurt, we show concern, like you.

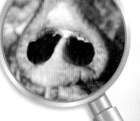

The African
elephant has
a very useful
and sensitive
trunk tip. This
tip is nimble
enough to turn
the pages of a book.

We love playing in watering holes.

It's easy to get hot and thirsty here in the
desert, so we travel in groups to find water. It is
said that elephants never forget. We make sure
we remember where water holes are so we can keep
going back to drink and squirt water over ourselves!

or watch baby elephants playing and bathing in the mud at www.arkive.org/african-elephant

Wild Bactrian camel

Guess what's inside my humps? Many people think they contain water, but it's actually fat. I'm the only two-humped camel in the world, and I live in parts of Mongolia and China. Although I can survive without water for a long time, it does make me thinner and weaker. I'm always looking for my next long drink!

Did you know?

We're named after an area where many of us live—Bactria, in northwest Asia.

I can run as fast as a horse.

I have a cousin in Africa, called the dromedary camel, who has just one hump.

We have thick pads on our knees to support our weight and protect us when we lie down.

When we can't find fresh water, some of us drink from saltwater sources instead. We are the only mammals who can do this!

We can take the heat.

By allowing our body temperature to rise by several degrees in hot weather, we save water since we don't need to sweat to cool ourselves down. There is little water, so we rarely urinate. Our eyelashes are long and our nostrils can close to keep out sandstorm dust.

A wild Bactrian camel has two toes on each foot. These spread out to help it walk in the desert. The padded soles of the camel's feet give protection from the hot sand.

 See the Bactrian camel by visiting the Wild Camel Protection Foundation at www.wildcamels.com

We're good swimmers.

Does that surprise you? I like to make the most of water when I find it. Herds of us travel together looking for water, and we can drink huge quantities if we're lucky enough to come across an oasis.

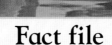

My winter coat is falling off!

We cope with the change from icy cold winters to swelteringly hot summers by shedding our shaggy coats. As the temperature soars, my fur falls off in big clumps. You can see piles of it on the ground.

Fact file

Asia

Pacific Ocean

Key
Wild Bactrian camels live here.

Population
= 1000

| 1980 | 3,000 |
| 2003 | fewer than 950 |

This type of camel is one of the world's rarest mammals. Its number is expected to drop by 80 percent in the near future.

Wild Bactrian camels under threat

 Hunting These camels are a target for hunters for both their meat and fur. Farmers sometimes hunt camels because they compete with their livestock for precious water and food.

 Habitat loss There are plans to develop the desert for different projects. A gas pipeline is planned that would cut through the homeland of these camels.

I followed my mom after 24 hours.

She was pregnant with me for more than a year before I was born in spring. I could walk within hours of being born and soon learned to keep close to Mom. She fed me her milk, which was more nutritious and lower in fat than cow's milk. I stayed with her for about two years.

Eating plumps up my humps.

When I'm eating well, I have large humps, but when there is a shortage of food, my humps get smaller and lean to the side. I survive on any branches, herbs, and grasses I can find.

I keep up to date with the weather. We can tell when rain has fallen, even some distance away. We make our way over because there will be new plants to eat.

Arabian oryx

Have you heard of the unicorn?

It's a mythical creature that looks like a white horse with a straight, long horn coming out of its forehead. Over the centuries, many people believed that we were unicorns! We are actually the smallest type of oryx antelope, and we have two long horns. Our home is hot desert in Arabia. Surviving in this harsh habitat isn't easy.

Did you know?

The last wild Arabian oryx was shot dead in 1972. The animals continued to live in captivity. Ten years later, the first captive herd was reintroduced into the wild.

Arab poets often wrote of the beauty and strength of the oryx.

We're slow runners, but we don't mind long-distance walking.

My body temperature can reach 113°F (45°C) without my overheating.

The large hooves of the Arabian oryx are like shovels. The ground is stony and bumpy, so the hooves spread out to make a wider area to walk on.

Can you see our horns growing?

When we're very young, you can only see the beginnings of our famous horns. My coat was brown when I was born, but it changed to white by the time I was three months old.

Our horns are the ultimate protection.

Both males and females have horns, but the female's horns are longer and thinner. We use them to defend ourselves against any newcomers. By lowering our heads, our horns point forward.

Find out more about the Arabian oryx from The Arabian Oryx Project at www.oryxoman.com

Our coats are bright white.
This means we can reflect the sun's rays instead of absorbing them. It's one way we keep cooler. Our white color also means that we blend in with the light landscape, so predators find us harder to see.

We make do with the bare minimum for dinner.
Like many of the animals here, we graze on grasses. We can go for long periods without water because the vegetation contains moisture. To avoid the heat, we dig into the ground and lie in the cooler sand.

It's hard to beat the heat.
The Arabian desert is unbearably hot, even in the shade. In summer, the temperature under the trees can reach 122°F (50°C). All we can do is stand here and move as little as possible.

Fact file

Key
Arabian oryx live here.

Red Sea

Asia

Population

= 150

The Arabian oryx continues to be one of the rarest mammals in the world.

1972 | the last known oryx in the wild was shot

2003 | fewer than 900

Arabian oryx under threat

Hunting Some travelers in Arabia used to hunt the oryx for meat and fur. In World War II, rifles and vehicles arrived in Arabia, and hunting increased. Laws to control hunting are now in place.

Drought This has made some of the land where the oryx live even drier, with less vegetation to eat.

or read the story of how the Arabian oryx was rescued at www.arkive.org/arabian-oryx

Gila monster

One bite from me could kill you.

I'm the largest lizard in the US, and I'm deadly poisonous. Home is the dry deserts of the Southwest. If I'm attacked, I bite my enemy. Poison flows into them through my grooved teeth, then I chew to drive the poison deep into the wound. I'm hard to shake, since my jaws clench so tight!

These eggs have just been laid. During summer, the females lay their eggs in a hole in the sand or inside a burrow. These eggs are oval-shaped and the shells feel like leather. Mothers don't stay to see their eggs hatch.

Eggs crack open in spring.

We are already brightly colored and about 6 in (15 cm) long when we first hatch from our eggs. By the time we're fully grown, about two years later, we are three times this length.

Did you know?

Our tails show how healthy we are. A fat tail means we are eating well, but a thin tail means we are hungry and thirsty.

We spend almost all of our time in or at the entrance to a burrow.

We are named after the Gila River Basin, where some of us live.

When we bite very hard, our teeth can get left behind in a wound.

My stomach is large, so I am able to eat a lot of food in a short time.

I'm not picky about my food.

Usually, I eat meat, but I'll snack on practically anything I find on the ground. As I move around looking for food, I flick out my tongue to detect any tasty treats. Eggs are my favorite, but I also enjoy munching on rats, lizards, birds, frogs, and insects.

Find out more by visiting Dr. Mark Seward's Gila monster website at www.drseward.com

Can you figure out where I am?

My skin blends in with the landscape, so my predators struggle to see me. I don't worry about being attacked, since I can unleash my poison. I'm often out of sight because I go underground to escape the heat.

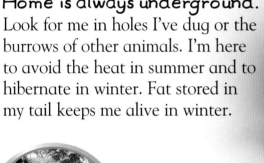

Home is always underground.

Look for me in holes I've dug or the burrows of other animals. I'm here to avoid the heat in summer and to hibernate in winter. Fat stored in my tail keeps me alive in winter.

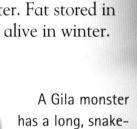

A Gila monster has a long, snake-like tongue. The tongue is forked and sensitive. It can taste the scents left behind by prey.

Fact file

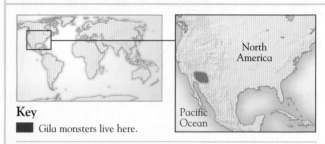

Key
■ Gila monsters live here.

Population

🦎 = 100

Population figures for Gila monsters are estimates. Numbers have never been recorded.

2004 | about 360

Gila monsters under threat

Habitat destruction Farmland and grazing animals have taken over much of this desert land. Roads have also cut across the habitat. Many Gila monsters are killed by domestic cats and dogs.

Pet trade Gila monsters are taken from the wild to be sold in the illegal pet trade.

I've got multicolored skin!

My hard, black skin is broken up with blotches of orange, pink, and yellow. If my predators see me when I'm above ground, these colors warn them to stay away. My sharp claws are also tough—I use them to dig my burrows.

Indian wild ass

Although I'm sand-colored like the desert, I stand out because I'm noisy and whiz around. I talk a lot, using a variety of sounds, including squeals, brays, and whinnies. I'm a fast runner—you wouldn't be able to keep up with me. I'm always on the go. I can even sleep standing up! My home is a tiny area of desert in India, and around here I'm known as a khur.

I like to roll in the dust.
When I get too hot, I roll on the ground. It also helps to keep my coat clean and my skin healthy. Once we know water is nearby, we can relax because we must drink every day.

We are born to run.
A few hours after I was born, I could run alongside my mom. That's because foals have long legs for their size. I also had a long, fleecy coat, but I shed this after a few weeks. Mom fed me her milk for eight months, and then I began to graze.

The Indian wild ass uses both upper and lower front teeth for tearing off grass and grooming. You can tell the age of an ass by looking at its front teeth.

Find out about wild asses from the Equid Specialist Group at www.iucn.org/themes/ssc/sgs/equid

We're fast enough to escape predators.

My long legs help me run fast, and I can maintain my speed. I don't get tired, so predators often give up chasing me. I also make a quick exit if I upset another ass. I know because their ears go back, their teeth show, and they try to bite my bottom!

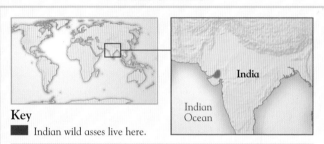

Fact file

Key

■ Indian wild asses live here.

India

Indian Ocean

Population

Although Indian wild asses are endangered, conservation areas are slowly helping to protect them.

= 500

| 1976 | | about 700 |
| 1999 | | about 2,800 |

Indian wild asses under threat

Hunting Asses are hunted for their meat and fur. Hunters also enjoy catching fast-moving animals.

Habitat loss People are intruding on the reserves that have been set up to protect the asses.

Disasters These asses live in a tiny area. A disease or a disaster, such as a drought, could kill them off.

Let me just get this itch.

That's better. There are insects in the desert that annoy us. We regularly have to groom ourselves and each other. We beat bugs by snapping at them or batting them off with a hind hoof.

Groups gather as herds.

We usually live in small groups. A dominant male has a territory, but will allow other males and passing females to live there. In the dry season, herds gather to share any available water source.

We feast during the night.

Since it's so hot during the day, I usually graze at dawn and dusk. If grass is available, it's my first choice. When it's very dry, we forage for twigs and leaves because that's all there is. They take a lot of chewing! My cheek teeth wear down, but they make up for it by continually growing.

Coral Pink Sand Dunes tiger beetle

I'm always on the lookout for my next meal. Here in the Coral Pink Sand Dunes of Utah, I spend the day looking for insects to eat. My powerful jaws can easily trap and bite them. I also eat any dead insects I come across. At night, I dig deep into the dunes to sleep.

 Off-road vehicles are popular in the area, but they destroy the dunes and kill beetles.

Desert watch

The heat and the shortage of water in the desert are a challenge for the animals living here. Vegetarian animals often get moisture from the plants they eat. Many of the animals, such as the greater bilby, burrow underground to escape the heat, so the desert can appear lifeless. Others, such as the saiga antelope, make the most of the shade by resting under the vegetation.

Greater bilby

I'm one of the best burrowers of the Australian deserts. With my sharp claws and fast digging, I can disappear into the sand very quickly. We build underground tunnels to escape the heat. After dusk, we come out to eat insects and vegetation. My rabbitlike ears help me hear insects nearby, and I lick them up with my long tongue!

Greater bilbies are hunted for their soft, silky fur.

Woma python

I'm also known as the sand python. I live in some of the driest parts of the Australian desert. It's so hot here that I only feed at night. My body is 8 ft (2.5 m) long, and I use it to force small mammals and lizards up against the side of their burrows and crush them to death. My scales were once smooth, but now they are scarred because my victims fight back!

 Some of the python's habitat has been converted into farmland.

Desert tortoise

The temperature soars above 140°F (60°C) where I live in the North American deserts. When it gets this hot, I spend a lot of my time in a burrow. Most of my water comes from moisture in the grass I eat. Although it rarely rains, we make the most of any rainfall. We dig basins in the sand and remember their location. If rain looks likely, we wait by the basins to drink the drops as they collect.

Housing, farmland, and mines have taken over the desert.

Saiga antelope

My huge, humped nose serves me well. It filters away dust during summer and heats up the air I breathe in cold winters. I also wear different coats throughout the year. My summer fur is beige and thin, but it turns white and becomes 70 percent thicker in winter. We live in central Asia, and groups of us leave the desert in summer to head for the grassland to feed.

 Males are hunted for their horns, to be used in medicine.

Northern hairy-nosed wombat

I'm one of the largest burrowing animals. To escape the Australian desert heat, I dig into the sand with my paws. It goes everywhere! That's why moms have pouches facing backward to protect their young from the flying sand while they're digging.

 Some of the habitat is now used as grazing land for domestic herds.

Humpback whale

Sea otter

Ocean

There are five oceans in the world, which cover two-thirds of Earth's surface. These oceans link together and have many rivers flowing into them. An amazing 80 percent of all life on Earth is found under the surface of the oceans. Many marine animals have flippers or fins, which they use to move through the water.

Ocean facts

● Scientists have names for at least 275,000 types of marine plants and animals.

● The largest ocean is the Pacific, with more than half the world's seawater.

● Ocean floors are not flat! There are undersea mountains and trenches.

● Waves are caused by wind blowing across the surface of the water. The height of the waves depends on the wind's strength.

Marine iguana

West Indian manatee

Green turtle

Threats to oceans

As coastal resorts become more developed and crowded, problems of pollution increase. Noise, boat traffic, and oil spills disturb the wildlife. Fishing nets and discarded plastics trap or drown many thousands of sea birds and marine animals every year.

Arctic Ocean

Europe

North America

Asia

Atlantic Ocean

Pacific Ocean

Pacific Ocean

Africa

South America

Indian Ocean

Australasia

Southern Ocean

Antarctic

Oceans of the World

Humpback whale

It's hard to miss us! We live in all the oceans and each of us is the size of a house. Every year, we migrate thousands of miles from the icy, polar waters where we feed to the warm, tropical seas where our babies are born. While swimming, the male whales sing loudly. A tune can last for 20 minutes, and you'll hear us singing it for hours. No wonder we're the noisiest whales!

A humpback whale has no teeth. Instead, comblike bristles called "baleen" hang from the top jaw. These strain prey from the water.

Babies weigh a ton.

I was never tiny like you. Within 10 seconds of my birth, Mom helped me to the surface to gulp my first breath of air. Just 30 minutes later, I had learned to swim! We're called "calves" when we're young. Calves survive by drinking their mother's milk for about the first year.

Did you know?

My heart weighs the same as three average-sized adult people.

We can live for up to 80 years.

Many of us have scars on our skins. When you're this big, you have to expect a few bumps and bruises!

The pattern on the underside of our tails is different for each of us.

Each whale can eat up to 1 ton of food a day.

Move aside if I'm breathing!

Otherwise, you'll get covered in spray! We come to the surface to breathe every 15 minutes. I have a double blowhole on my head, and this does the same job as your nostrils.

It's quite a scene at feeding time.

First we form a circle underwater. Then we blow a wall of bubbles as we swim to the surface. These bubbles act as a net to trap big groups of fish and move them upward. We swim to the surface with our mouths wide open to gorge on the feast.

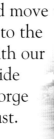

To find out more, visit the Whale and Dolphin Conservation Society at www.wdcs.org

I'm one of the ocean's great performers.

Here I am playing around. Look at my flippers. They are longer than the flippers of any other type of whale. We live in groups called "pods," and we have lots of fun. Playing, traveling, and feeding are all shared activities.

I'm known for my spectacular leaps.

I love to throw myself right out of the water. Sometimes I even twirl around like an acrobat as I surge through the air. If there are any boats nearby, the people on board get a free show!

Fact file

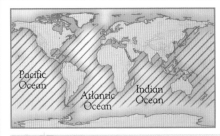

Key

/// Humpback whales live here.

Humpback whales migrate, which is why they are found in all the oceans.

Population

 = 15,000

Since 1965, the humpback whale population has fallen by more than half.

| 1965 | fewer than 75,000 |
| 2004 | fewer than 28,000 |

Humpback whales under threat

 Hunting Even though it is illegal, people continue to hunt humpback whales.

 Fishing nets Whales become entangled in fishing nets and drown.

 Pollution Oil spills and water pollution can kill humpback whales.

You'll see my huge tail when I dive deep.

As I go into a dive, I arch my back and my tail rises out of the water. Stay clear, though—it's 18 ft (5.5 m) wide! Fish move their tails from side to side, but we move ours up and down.

Sea otter

I'm a real water baby. With my sleek flippers and rudderlike tail, I can't fail to be a superb swimmer. I have no blubber, so my fur coat keeps me cozy in the chilly Pacific Ocean. I'm often seen grooming myself and rolling around in the water because it traps air in my fur. This air keeps my skin dry and warm, while I stay looking good!

The sea otter has the thickest fur of all animals. An adult sea otter has 650,000 hairs on an area the size of a postage stamp.

Did you know?

Our mothers stop grooming us when we are about two months old. At this age, we start learning to dive.

When we're searching for food, we can recognize and avoid any poisonous shellfish.

The fur on our heads is the color of straw, but it looks silver when wet.

Many males defend a territory. Any disagreements are settled by splashing and shouting at each other.

Do-it-yourself makes eating easy. We are one of the few animals in the world who use tools. We find rocks and pebbles and use them to break open shells. So don't be alarmed if you hear the sound of smashing coming from the sea!

I enjoy my seafood platter. Here I am digging in to a starfish. I also love to dine on sea urchins, clams, crabs, mussels, and sea snails. The ocean offers lots of variety, so I can look forward to a different dish every day.

Learn about a sea otter sanctuary by visiting Friends of the Sea Otter at www.seaotters.org

Now we've made the bed, it's time to sleep.

There is a type of seaweed along the coastline called kelp. If we throw lots of kelp over us, it stops us from drifting away. That means we can rest and relax, while floating. We lie back on the kelp and even fall asleep if we get too comfortable!

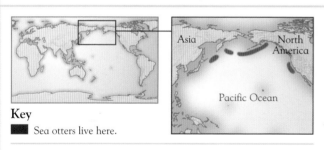

Fact file

Key

███ Sea otters live here.

Asia · North America · Pacific Ocean

Population

🦦 = 15,000

Although sea otter populations have grown over the last century, they are still at risk.

| 1911 | 🦦 fewer than 2,000 |
| 2004 | 🦦 🦦 🦦 🦦 🦦 🦦 fewer than 90,000 |

Sea otters under threat

 Hunting In the past, sea otters were hunted because their fur was used to make clothing.

 Oil spills Accidents kill huge numbers of sea otters. In 1989, an oil spill in Alaska killed 2,650.

 Fishing nets Sea otters get accidentally caught up in nets that are meant to trap fish.

Babies have yellow fur.

It gradually turns brown as they get older. Young sea otters like this are called "pups". Mothers spend a long time grooming their pups. As a result, pup fur traps so much air that they can only float!

I'm going shopping.

I swim around underwater, looking for tempting food to eat. It's my own supermarket down here. Under my arms are pouches of loose skin, which I use to carry my food. I surface to breathe and then munch on all the goodies I've found.

Marine iguana

When you look at my tough, scaly skin, you might not be too surprised to find out that I'm related to the dinosaurs.

I use my strong claws to clamber around the cliffs of the Galápagos Islands, which are my home. I don't know about dinosaurs, but my seaweed diet can make me turn red or green.

The marine iguana has a crest of scales that run down its back. These scales are a protective layer over the iguana's skin.

There's never a dull moment

So many other island dwellers hang out on the rocks that it get pretty crowded, especially when the sun comes out! With lizards, crabs, sea lions, and birds, there i always someone to see.

Did you know?

When we're very hungry, we don't just get thinner— we actually get shorter, too!

We male iguanas like to show off with displays of head-bobbing.

We are the only reptiles known to eat seaweed.

Explorer and naturalist Charles Darwin described us as "hideous in appearance, sluggish, stupid, and ugly." A little harsh, don't you think?

I'm a sun-worshipper.

Sunrise is my cue to soak up the rays. I climb out from the crevice where I've been sleeping and head for the cliffs. This is where I spend the day on the rocks we share with crabs, like this one. We're cold-blooded creatures, so our bodies need heat to keep warm. These islands are perfect sun-traps.

Find out more about marine iguanas by visiting the Galápagos Conservation Trust at www.gct.org/

I love a dip in the ocean.
It is only us larger iguanas who swim. My flattened tail helps me go faster. Usually, I'm underwater for five minutes, but I can stay under for an hour, swimming at depths of up to 80 ft (25 m).

I like seaweed for supper.
When it's time to eat, I always head for the shore. My body is in tune with the tides. I know when it is low tide, and that's when I go and munch away on the exposed seaweed.

We grow up on our own.
Once the mother iguanas have laid their eggs in the volcanic ash found here, they guard them for up to two weeks and then leave. The eggs hatch about three months later. Although our parents don't take care of us, our natural instincts help us survive.

Fact file

Key
Marine iguanas live here.

Pacific Ocean

South America

Galápagos Islands

Population = 100,000

2004 | 300,000

The most recent population figure is estimated at fewer than 300,000. The first marine iguanas probably floated over on driftwood from South America.

Marine iguanas under threat

Hunting Humans have introduced cats, dogs, and rats to the Galápagos Islands. These all hunt young marine iguanas and eat their eggs. New populations of marine iguanas are then reduced.

Marine pollution An oil spill in 2001 killed 15,000 iguanas. Scientists think oil kills the bacteria that iguanas need to digest their food. Many iguanas die as a result.

West Indian manatee

In the past, people have mistaken us for mermaids.

That was probably from a distance, though! I think we look more like walruses, but we are actually more closely related to the elephant. With our thick, gray skin, enormous bodies, and constant munching, we've certainly got a lot in common!

Hey, Mom, are you listening to me?

Most of the talking you'll hear underwater is between mothers and babies. We make high-pitched noises similar to the sounds of dolphins. Like all manatees, I stayed with Mom for the first two years of my life.

We play together underwater.

Doing somersaults in the warm water is a lot of fun. We're excellent swimmers because our flippers are flexible and our tails are big. Our lungs are as long as our bodies, so we can stay underwater for five minutes at a time.

Plants wear down my teeth.

The tough plants I eat are very hard on my teeth. Luckily, my teeth replace themselves. The worn ones fall out at the front of my mouth, while the new ones move forward from the back.

Did you know?

We have split upper lips. Both parts can move around separately, and this helps us to eat the seagrass.

As a result of how slowly we move, barnacles attach themselves to our skin, just like they do to the underside of boats.

We breathe through our nostrils, which close up when we're underwater.

Many of us have scars on our bodies where boats have collided with us.

I'm known as the sea cow.

The only difference between a land cow's diet and mine is that I forage underwater to find my dinner. Every day, I graze on lots of seagrass and water plants like this one. My daily menu would be the same as your eating 200 lettuces!

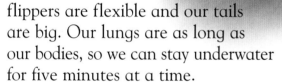

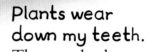

You can help the manatees by visiting Save the Manatee Club at www.savethemanatee.org

I'm such a romantic!
Although I spend most of my time swimming alone, I'm usually friendly when I meet other manatees. We're very gentle and relaxed with one another. Sometimes we nuzzle up together.

The manatee has a large paddle-shaped tail, used for swimming and balance. Strong up-and-down tail strokes propel it through the water.

Fact file

Key

■ West Indian manatees live here.

Atlantic Ocean

South America

Population

🦭 = 5,000

2004 | 🦭🦭 about 10,000

There are no definite population figures for manatees. An estimate in 2004 showed fewer than 10,000. Aerial surveys are used to gather data about manatees.

West Indian manatees under threat

Boat traffic The increasing numbers of boats colliding with manatees are the biggest threat to their survival.

Habitat loss Coastal development has brought tourists, who use the beaches and sea for leisure activities.

Hunting New protection laws have reduced this threat.

Pollution Water pollution destroys the sea plants eaten by manatees.

Instead of sleepwalking, we sleepswim!
We don't have any natural predators, so it's safe for us to rest or take a nap on the sea floor. However, we do have to come up to the surface to breathe. We get so relaxed down here that we're often still half-asleep when we reach the surface.

Green turtle

I am the Christopher Columbus of the turtle world. My long-distance travel and exploration are well known. Don't be surprised if you find me anywhere in any ocean, as long as the temperature doesn't fall below a comfortable 68°F (20°C). Like you, I prefer to swim in warm waters. Our mothers migrate thousands of miles across the ocean just to lay their eggs!

Did you know?

Some female green turtles nest on Ascension Island in the Atlantic Ocean, then travel back 1,400 miles (2,250 km) to feed in Brazil's waters.

One seagrass is called "turtle grass" because we eat so much of it!

In 1503, Christopher Columbus saw two islands full of turtles. He described them as looking like rocks, but they were really green turtles!

My name refers to the green coloring of my body fat.

Females return to the beach of their birth. That can be quite a distance. But this is the only place they will lay their eggs. They use their flippers to clear the sand and make a hole. They lay about 100 eggs, cover the hole with sand, and return to the sea.

I don't need a map of the sea floor. That's because I know the exact location of the places I've visited before. We turtles return to the same spots to feed or breed. Our streamlined flippers help us to swim around quickly.

Find out more about traveling turtles by visiting Turtle Trax at www.turtles.org

It's a dangerous dash to the sea.
Two months after the female lays her eggs, they hatch. Babies then have to dig their way out of the sand and hurry down the beach to the sea. I remember hungry crabs and birds waiting to eat us along the way. It's a scary way to start life. Sadly, many of us don't survive.

We're friendly turtles.
There's a lot of playing, swimming, and feeding together along the reefs. Rocks and coral are our beds, and we gather together for a nap. We sometimes have squabbles and fights, though. That's when we swim away on our own to calm down.

The green turtle has flippers that work well in this underwater world. They are strong and shaped like paddles to move easily through the water.

Fish are our own personal cleaners!
When our shells get grimy, we don't use soap like you. We have fish here who do the cleaning! There are many cleaner fish in the ocean, and we swim over to where they live. They pick the algae and dead skin off us and eat them.

Fact file

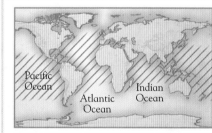

Pacific Ocean

Atlantic Ocean

Indian Ocean

Key
/// Green turtles live here.

Green turtles live in many oceans of the world. They travel long distances to nest and feed.

Population

= 50,000

There are no total population numbers available for the green turtle. Scientists have estimated that there are more than 203,000 breeding female green turtles.

2003 | 🐢 🐢 🐢 🐢   more than 203,000

Green turtles under threat

Hunting Although green turtles are supposed to be protected, hunting continues. Turtle parts are used to make leather, cosmetics, and turtle soup.

Coastal development The increasing number of seaside resorts is reducing the places where green turtles can go to lay their eggs.

Leafy seadragon

Am I a seadragon or seaweed? It's hard to tell. I'm a great example of ocean camouflage. My leaflike appearance helps me blend in with the Australian coral reefs. I move gently, like swaying seaweed, so you'd have to look very closely to see my tiny eyes and clear fins.

 Coastal resorts pollute and disturb the habitat.

Ocean watch

Marine animals live in a range of different habitats, from rocky coasts and coral reefs to seaweed forests and the dark waters near the sea floor. Wherever they live, avoiding predators is their main concern. Many animals, including the leafy seadragon, blend in so well with their surroundings that they are difficult to see. Others, like the Hector's dolphin, swim in groups to make them safer from attack.

Great white shark

Any huge, dark shadow lurking underwater could be me. Nothing living here eats me—I'm at the top of the ocean food chain. I cruise around the warm waters of the world looking for seals, turtles, and fish to eat. The top of my body is very dark, so I merge in with the deep water. When my prey is swimming above me, they don't know I'm there until it's too late!

 These sharks are hunted as a sport and for their fins.

Wandering albatross

I'm as well-traveled as my name suggests. Most of my time is spent soaring high above the open ocean. My wings are larger than any other bird's. They stretch farther than the width of a bus! With my wings outstretched and still, I can glide effortlessly along on the wind. Here, I'm dancing in a courtship ceremony with my mate. When we meet a mate, we stay together for life.

 These birds often drown on the end of fishing hooks when they try to eat the bait from fishing boats.

Whale shark

If you saw me swimming in your direction, you'd probably feel terrified! Although I'm the largest fish in the ocean, and my mouth is 5 ft (1.5 m) wide, I'm not the least bit interested in eating you. In fact, my favorite food is small fish and plankton. I keep my mouth open as I swim through the tropical waters, straining the water and gulping down large quantities of fish.

Whale shark meat is eaten in parts of Asia.

Hector's dolphin

If you were swimming off the coast of New Zealand where I live, I would come and investigate. I'm the smallest dolphin in the sea, and I'm very curious about people. I love company and lots of my time is spent playing games with other dolphins. We jump out of the water, swim around in the surf, play with seaweed, and blow big, tickly bubbles underwater.

Dolphins get caught up in fishing nets.

Manta ray

You might think you see a giant blanket floating along in the tropics, but it's me! The word *manto* is Spanish for "cloak," and that's exactly what I look like. As the largest ray of all, I cause quite a stir when I go by. My huge fins flap to power me along. I'm quite an athlete—sometimes I jump right out of the water!

Manta rays are hunted for their liver and skin, to be used in cleaning products.

Cheetah

Black rhinoceros

Grassland

![grass] This landscape is dominated by different types of grasses. Tropical grasslands, called savannas, are found in warm or hot climates where all the rain falls in six to eight months of the year. This is followed by a long period of drought. Temperate grasslands have less rainfall with hot summers and cold winters.

Grassland facts

● **National parks** have been set up in many countries to protect the grasslands and the different animals living there.

● **In Africa,** elephants are causing environmental damage in the limited space of the national parks. Elephants are knocking down all the trees, so the woodland is turning into grassland.

● **Grasslands are known** by a variety of names in different countries. Other names include prairie, plains, and pampas.

Hyacinth macaw

Grevy's zebra

Giant anteater

Threats to grasslands

Since grasslands are often rich in nutrients and good for growing crops, people have turned much of them into farmland. This means there is less room for the animals. Also, domestic herds eat so much that grasses do not grow back.

Grasslands of the World

Cheetah

If all the land animals in the world had a race, I'd win.

I am faster than any of them because I'm built for speed. My legs are very long and powerful, and my spine is stretchy and flexible. I also have huge nostrils so I can fill my lungs with extra air. The length of my tail ensures that I stay balanced when moving at top speed. The African grasslands are vast, and I love racing around— especially if I spot something tasty!

Cubs have manes. Soft, white fuzz covers the heads and backs of cubs but disappears as they grow up. My cubs sometimes follow me on hunts, but they don't take part. I'll stay with them until they're full-grown at 18 months.

Did you know?

The fastest speed I can reach is 70 mph (112 km/h). I can't keep this up for long because I would overheat.

In one stride I can cover 23 ft (7 m).

Akbar the Great of India was said to have kept 1,000 cheetahs. Cheetahs used to live in India. The last one of us there died in 1952.

The name "cheetah" is from an Indian word meaning "spotted one."

We can growl, hiss, and chirrup.

We hunt when the heat's on. Although it's tiring to chase prey during the day with the temperature soaring, it's worth the extra effort. We avoid the leopards and lions who prefer to hunt at night. They want the same food as we do, so it's better not to compete. I need to kill about once a day to feed my family.

Find out more about cheetahs by visiting the Cheetah Conservation Fund at www.cheetah.org

Catch me if you can.

My feet hardly touch the ground when I'm sprinting. It looks like I'm about to take off! My spotted fur blurs at full speed. If you see me running like this, I'm usually chasing prey.

Fact file

Key
■ Cheetahs live here.

Atlantic Ocean

Africa

Population

🐆 = 10,000

Over the last century, cheetah populations have declined by nearly 90 percent.

1900	🐆🐆🐆🐆🐆🐆🐆🐆🐆🐆	100,000
2004	🐆🐆	fewer than 12,500

Cheetahs under threat

Lack of food Cheetahs living in protected parks must compete with the other big cats and hyenas for food. Often, the cheetahs are unsuccessful.

Low survival rate Most cubs don't live to be two years old because lions attack them.

Traps Cheetahs have attacked farm animals. Farmers have set traps in response.

I can outrun all my prey.

This time, my target is a gazelle. After stalking one, I chase it and knock it to the ground. Then I take a killer bite from the throat. I rest and get my breath back before eating my dinner.

A cheetah is the only cat that can't draw in its claws. They are used like spiked running shoes to provide a good grip for sprinting.

My family has a lot to learn.

The grasslands are a dangerous place, especially since lions kill our cubs. I make sure mine are hidden away before I go hunting. I bring them live prey to teach them how to chase and kill. If my cubs sense danger or they want to explore, they sometimes climb trees together.

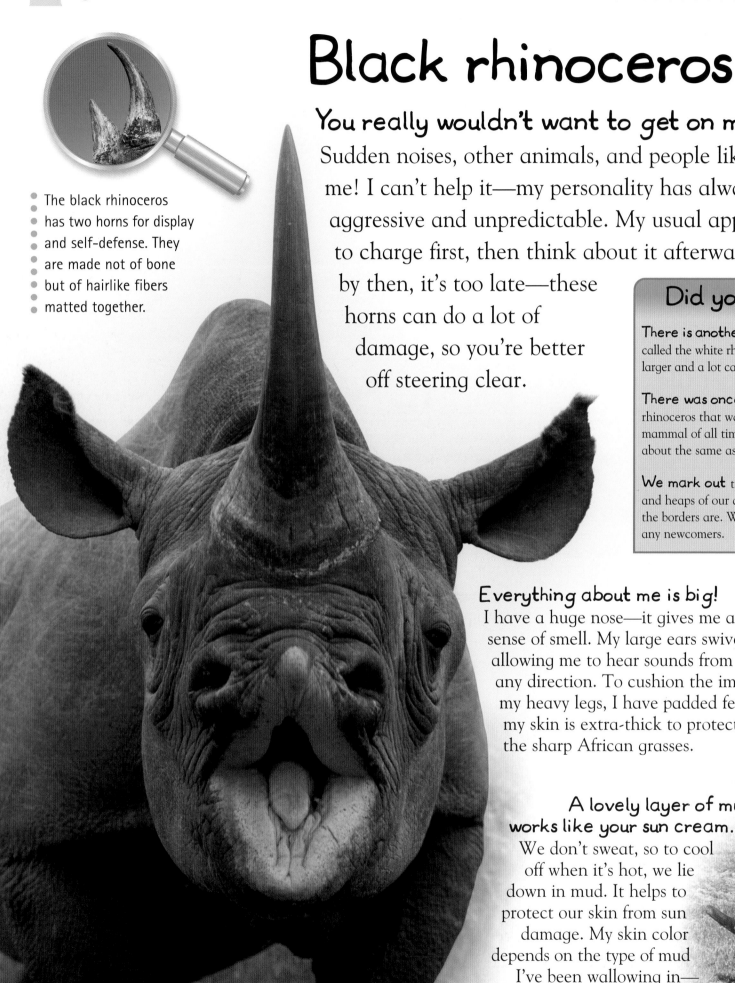

The black rhinoceros has two horns for display and self-defense. They are made not of bone but of hairlike fibers matted together.

Black rhinoceros

You really wouldn't want to get on my nerves. Sudden noises, other animals, and people like you annoy me! I can't help it—my personality has always been aggressive and unpredictable. My usual approach is to charge first, then think about it afterward. But by then, it's too late—these horns can do a lot of damage, so you're better off steering clear.

Did you know?

There is another type of rhinoceros called the white rhinoceros. They are larger and a lot calmer than we are!

There was once a type of rhinoceros that was the largest land mammal of all time. This type weighed about the same as four male elephants.

We mark out territories with urine and heaps of our dung to show where the borders are. We try to scare away any newcomers.

Everything about me is big! I have a huge nose—it gives me a terrific sense of smell. My large ears swivel around, allowing me to hear sounds from almost any direction. To cushion the impact of my heavy legs, I have padded feet. Even my skin is extra-thick to protect me from the sharp African grasses.

A lovely layer of mud works like your sun cream. We don't sweat, so to cool off when it's hot, we lie down in mud. It helps to protect our skin from sun damage. My skin color depends on the type of mud I've been wallowing in—I can be gray, brown, or red!

Find out more by visiting the International Rhino Foundation at www.rhinos-irf.org

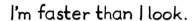

I'm faster than I look.
If you hear loud snorting, you'd better watch out. It could be me on the move or even charging. Although I'm heavy, I can reach a top speed of 30 mph (50 km/h).

These birds keep my skin clean.
My skin is covered in nasty bugs, but I can't always get at them. Luckily for me, birds like this oxpecker live here, too. They sit on me and peck the bugs off my skin. Everybody's happy because they get a good meal and I stay healthy.

It's true — I've always been enormous.
Even when I was born, I was 12 times heavier than you were. Within hours, I was active. In fact, just three days later I was following Mom around. She taught me where to look for plants to eat.

Fact file

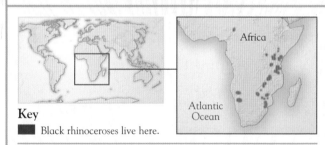

Africa

Atlantic Ocean

Key

■ Black rhinoceroses live here.

Population

🦏 = 10,000

The black rhinoceros was hunted during the 1970s and 1980s, as the figures show.

1970 | 🦏🦏🦏🦏🦏🦏🦏 65,000
2004 | 🦏 about 3,600

Black rhinoceroses under threat

⊕ **Hunting** Black rhinoceroses are hunted for their horns. Some people grind up the horn to use as a medicine. People also use the horn to make fancy handles for daggers.

🚜 **Land development** The land where black rhinoceroses live has been cleared for farming.

or watch a baby rhinoceros and its mother grazing at www.arkive.org/black-rhinoceros
 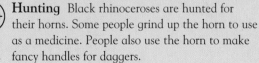 55

Hyacinth macaw

As I fly over the South American grasslands, you'll see a bright flash of brilliant blue.

I'm renowned for my flamboyant coloring. You certainly can't miss me because I'm also the biggest parrot in the world—as tall as a five-year-old child. If I fly a bit too close, it's because I'm nosy. I want to take a good look at you. Why don't you try talking to me? I might try to mimic your voice!

We're very messy eaters.
Trees like this are our restaurants. We love nuts, fruit, and seeds. While we're eating or carrying food away in our beaks, we often drop seeds on the ground. So our mess is the reason new palm trees spring up all over the place!

Don't eat my dinner—it could kill you!
We can eat poisonous seeds that are harmful to other animals. The secret is the clay in the rivers here. You'll find flocks of us munching away on this clay, which absorbs the poisons in the food we're eating.

I'm a fearless flyer.
I've been able to fly since I was three months old. We fly in flocks of about five pairs of macaws. We make loud, screeching calls as we fly—this keeps us in close contact and ensures that we don't lose each other. We can fly as fast as 35 mph (56 km/h)!

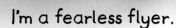 Visit WWF – Brazil's Hyacinth Macaw Project at www.wwf.org.br/english/informa/sitearara_arara.htm

Here I am!

My beak comes in very handy. I used it to dig a hole inside this tree. I prefer to expand on a hole already made by a woodpecker, or I choose a soft tree so the wood is easy to peck away. The hole is a perfect place for my family to shelter inside.

Fact file

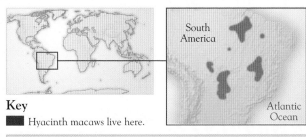

Key
■ Hyacinth macaws live here.

Population
 = 5,000

2003 | fewer than 10,000

The number of hyacinth macaws in the wild could be anywhere between 2,500 and 10,000. During the 1980s, about 10,000 birds were taken for the pet trade.

Hyacinth macaws under threat

Habitat loss These birds mainly eat two different types of palm nuts. When trees are cleared, food becomes scarce and the birds are unable to feed their young.

Pet trade Hyacinth macaws are easy to capture because they are noisy and have no fear of people.

Poor breeders Female macaws do not produce chicks every year.

We pair up together, forever.

Once we've found a partner, we stick together and raise our family. Females usually lay two eggs at a time, but often only one baby survives. It would be a rare thing to see a lone macaw. We love being with other macaws, and we enjoy your company, too!

The treetops get crowded.

After we've been flying around in groups, we settle to feed or have a rest up in the trees. We can grip the branches easily, thanks to our special feet. Two toes face forward and two face backward. This helps us keep our balance.

The heavy, curved beak of the hyacinth macaw is used to break the shells of tough nuts and seeds that would otherwise be impossible to crack open and eat.

or see hyacinth macaws using their feet to eat nuts at www.arkive.org/hyacinth-macaw

Grevy's zebra

Can you see my tummy?
It's mostly white, and that makes it the only part of me that isn't striped. You can see it when I'm rolling around getting the pesky flies off me.

I look like a horse, except I appear to be wearing striped pajamas. My stripes are thinner than the stripes on any other type of zebra. They protect me in the African grasslands. If I'm hiding behind bushes, my black-and-white coloring breaks up the outline of my body, making it hard for predators to spot me. I wouldn't be without my safety stripes!

It's safer to drink in a crowd.
Water supplies are few and far between. When we're thirsty, a group of males and females gather at a water source. Our stripes mingle together, so predators can't single out any of us to attack.

Did you know?

Although groups of lions hunt us, we are often able to outrun them over a long distance.

The king of Ethiopia gave the president of France, Jules Grevy, a gift of some zebras. This is how we got our name.

When I'm standing still at night, my stripes make me virtually invisible.

Baby zebras are usually born after a big rainfall. There is plenty of fresh grass to eat at this time.

I'm no pushover.
Most other zebras and horses live in herds, but we prefer our own company. Adult males like me have our own territory, where females pass through. Sometimes, another male will try to take my land. We rear up, shove, and bite each other—but I haven't lost a fight yet.

Find out more about Grevy's zebras at www.ultimateungulate.com/Perissodactyla/Equus_grevyi.html

Fact file

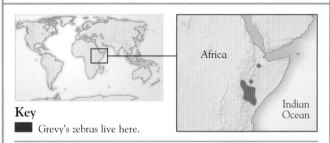

Africa

Indian Ocean

Key

◼ Grevy's zebras live here.

Population

 = 5,000

The number of Grevy's zebras has declined as a result of hunting and land clearance.

1987 🦓🦓🦓 fewer than 15,000

1993 🦓 fewer than 5,000

Grevy's zebras under threat

⊕ **Hunting** During the 1970s, the zebra's unusual fur became popular as fashionable clothing.

🚜 **Habitat loss** Grasslands are being cleared to make farmland. The remaining zebras living there must compete with the farm herds for grass and water.

We get along with our neighbors.

Here in the grasslands, we live in harmony with other animals. Ostriches, antelopes, and wildebeest graze with us. There's no trouble until a lion comes on the scene. Then you should see how quickly we disappear!

I was a fast learner.

Half an hour after I was born, I could walk. Within an hour, I could run. I already knew my mom by either seeing or smelling her. Not bad for an hour's work!

The long ears of the Grevy's zebra pick up sounds in the far distance. They also rotate to determine the direction of a sound.

I bray like a donkey.

This is how zebras talk to each other. We like to show our teeth! The front ones clip the grass, and the back teeth chew it up. Can you see my tongue? It's very sensitive and can sense even the slightest difference in the quality of the grass I eat.

or take a look at a young Grevy's zebra being nursed by its mother at www.arkive.org/grevys-zebra ✉

Giant anteater

I'm a bit like a vacuum cleaner. But instead of sucking up dirt, I swallow 30,000 ants every single day. I flick my long tongue in and out so fast that the ants don't stand a chance. In fact, I can chomp my way through several thousand of them in just a few minutes. I don't have teeth, so I can't chew my food. Instead, I swallow pebbles, which help to crush the ants inside my tummy.

Can you see where my head is?
I usually sleep out in the open, but my tail makes me hard to see. Eating ants doesn't provide me with enough energy to do much, so I save energy by sleeping up to 15 hours a day.

A giant anteater has a tongue that can be as long as your arm. It is covered in sticky saliva and small spines to extract prey from nests and mounds.

Did you know?

At 90°F (32°C), we have the lowest body temperature of all mammals on land.

We can identify ants with large, biting jaws so we avoid eating them.

We flick our tongues in and out approximately 150 times a minute.

When we feel threatened and there is no escape, we rear up on our back legs and lash out with our claws.

My sense of smell is much sharper than yours.
Once I've sniffed out a termite mound, I figure out who lives there. I can tell which type of termite it is by the smell. My strong legs and tough claws can rip open the mounds.

Find out about giant anteaters by visiting The Online Anteater at www.maiaw.com/anteater

These ants look mouthwatering.

I remember this type of ant—it's delicious. We only feed on an ant nest for a short time because we don't want to destroy it. Then we move on and return another time.

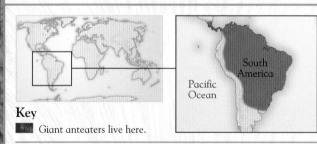

Seeing me drink is unusual.

I hardly ever drink because the ants I eat contain enough moisture already. This river is nearby, and I sometimes come for a swim. I'm a strong swimmer and am not afraid of getting wet.

Sometimes I have to work hard to find my food.

To give you an idea of the size of this termite mound, just consider that I'm 7 ft (2 m) long! Luckily, I am strong enough to climb to the top and stick my long nose in to sniff out the termites.

Babies enjoy a nine-month piggyback!

Moms carry babies on their backs when they go walking, usually to find ant nests. The baby blends in well with its mother's hair, so you'd hardly notice it was there. The baby sprawls out during the ride, clinging with its sharp claws, and spends most of the time asleep.

Fact file

Key
Giant anteaters live here.

Pacific Ocean

South America

Population

No numbers are available, but scientists think there has been an 80 percent reduction in population over the last 10 years.

1994

2004

Giant anteaters under threat

Fires Every three years, grasslands in Brazil burn naturally, and many giant anteaters are killed. In addition, some people deliberately start fires.

Habitat loss Vast areas of habitat have been destroyed by people. Giant anteaters are now largely restricted to living in national parks.

or see a baby anteater riding on its mother's back at www.arkive.org/giant-anteater

Grassland watch

All the animals in this habitat are alert because it is home to terrifying predators, such as cheetahs, coyotes, and wild dogs. Most of the smaller inhabitants are quick-thinking and fast on their feet. Many, such as prairie dogs, spend time in underground burrows to avoid attack. Birds, such as the great Indian bustard, have long legs to help them get a clear view above the grass.

Mexican prairie dog

It's fair to say that I'm carrying some extra weight! I store this fat for winter. We live in burrows and take turns guarding them. If we sense danger, we squeal to warn everyone to get inside. Coyotes, hawks, and badgers are all cause for big squeals!

 Land has been cleared for cattle and farming.

 Cats and foxes hunt these wallabies.

Rufous hare wallaby

Part of my scientific name means "dancing hare"—and that's not far from the truth. In appearance, movement, and size, I am a lot like a hare. However, my hind legs are longer and stronger, so I bop and hop around the Australian grasslands at great speed.

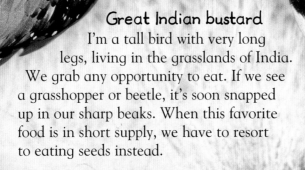

Great Indian bustard

I'm a tall bird with very long legs, living in the grasslands of India. We grab any opportunity to eat. If we see a grasshopper or beetle, it's soon snapped up in our sharp beaks. When this favorite food is in short supply, we have to resort to eating seeds instead.

 Areas where the bustards live have become farmland.

African wild dog

I'm the same size as an average pet dog. I live in the African grasslands, and my name means "painted wolf" in Latin. That's because my fur is a mixture of black, white, and yellow. Unlike domestic dogs, I have four toes on each front paw instead of five. We have bundles of energy and can run after antelopes and zebras for an hour. It's worth it when we catch one!

 Much of the habitat of the African wild dogs has been cleared. They now live in parks and reserves, but have less space.

Takahe

I'm a bird who can't fly. I use my brightly colored wings to show aggression or to attract the ladies. Although I'm blue and green with a red beak, I was born completely black. We only get our colors as we grow older. Between 1800 and 1900, there were only four sightings of us in our native New Zealand, so people assumed we were extinct. We were first seen again in 1948, and a conservation area was set up for us.

 Takahes have to compete for land with the red deer that have been introduced to the habitat.

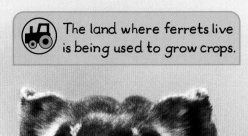 The land where ferrets live is being used to grow crops.

Black-footed ferret

I'm a member of the weasel family. Much of my time is spent in burrows under the North American grasslands. At night, I ferret around the burrows of prairie dogs because I want to eat them. We have excellent senses of smell, hearing, and eyesight. It's just as well, because owls, hawks, and badgers are eager to eat us.

Giant panda

Ethiopian wolf

Mountain

 Any land higher than 2,000 ft (600 m) is mountainous.

A mountain often forms when two pieces of Earth's crust collide. The land is pushed upward to form rocky peaks. From the snow-capped peaks to the trees and meadows lower down, there is an enormous variety of wildlife. Many animals have thick fur to keep them warm.

Mountain facts

- **Mount Everest** in the Himalayas is the world's highest mountain. The name Himalayas means "land of the snow."

- **The Andes** in South America is the longest continuous mountain range in the world.

- **About 80 percent** of the world's fresh water comes from the mountains.

- **More than a billion** people already live in the mountains.

Mountain gorilla

Snow leopard

Spectacled bear

Threats to mountains

Once wild and isolated, many mountain areas are now used by people. Ski resorts and snow sports damage the landscape, while more land on the lower slopes is taken over for farming. People have built roads and pipelines that cut through mountain ranges.

Arctic Ocean

North America

Europe

Asia

Atlantic Ocean

Pacific Ocean

Pacific Ocean

Africa

South America

Indian Ocean

Australasia

Southern Ocean

Antarctic

☐ Mountains of the World

Giant panda

I look soft and cuddly, don't I?

But if you touched me, you'd be surprised to find that my coat feels oily. I live high up in the mountains of China, and this natural oil is a protective coating on my fur to keep out the moisture on these rainy slopes.

The giant panda has an extra long wrist bone. This special bone is very useful when feeding on bamboo.

Bamboo is delicious.

There's enough bamboo here to fill me up. It's a tall, woody plant and it makes up 99 percent of my diet. I can munch my way through 90 lb (40 kg) a day.

Did you know?

Chinese people call us "da xiong mao" which means "giant bear cat" in their language. We are seen as a symbol of peace in this country.

We have excellent eyesight.

Our stomachs are specially designed to protect us from the splinters in bamboo.

Baby pandas are born white. The black markings on our fur only appear as we get a little older.

I don't look like a typical athlete.

Don't be fooled, though. My short claws cling easily to tree bark. If I sense danger, I climb a tree or swim away if I'm near a river. You might spot me up in a tree taking a snooze or admiring the amazing views.

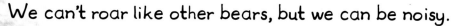
We can't roar like other bears, but we can be noisy.
Our conversation revolves around different sounds that we all use and understand. But we often sit in silence because we're so busy eating! We communicate by leaving scent and scratch marks on trees, too.

Fact file

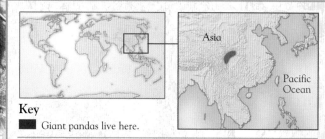

Key

■ Giant pandas live here.

Population

= 200

The rise may be the result of 2004's more detailed survey, rather than an increase in numbers.

1988		1,100
2004		1,600

Giant pandas under threat

Deforestation Between 1974 and 1989, the habitat of giant pandas shrank by half.

Increased human population New settlements create barriers, so pandas can't move around freely.

Hunting Illegal poaching continues because panda fur sells for a lot of money.

Here I am nodding off.
An afternoon nap in a tree is enough to prepare me for the tough task of eating more bamboo. We don't have a home like you, but when it's time to sleep, we have plenty of choices—there are trees, stumps, and rocks all around us in the mountains.

I weighed about as much as a tomato when I was born.
All cubs are tiny when they're born. I cried if I was hungry or wanted Mom, just like you did as a baby. My eyes opened at six weeks, and I began exploring. I loved to tumble around the hills.

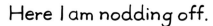

Ethiopian wolf

As the sun rises over the mountains of Ethiopia, you'll hear my howl echoing across the land. We're the only wolves in Africa and we hang around in large groups known as "packs." We greet each other with growls of excitement, and if a pack gathers together, howling can be heard up to 3 miles (5 km) away. It's just as loud if we sense danger. We raise the alarm with a series of loud yelps and barks.

The teeth of an Ethiopian wolf are small, with wide gaps between them. This helps the wolf to kill its prey, tear off the meat, and cut through it.

Did you know?

We're the most endangered member of the dog family in the world.

My pointed ears provide me with the great sense of hearing I need to pick up on members of the pack calling me from far away.

Male wolves stay with the pack, but female wolves leave when they are full-grown.

Apart from Ethiopia, we're not found anywhere else in the world.

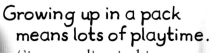

Growing up in a pack means lots of playtime. Since we live in big groups, pups always have others to play with. By the time I was three months old, my fur had turned from gray to red, my teeth were growing, and food had replaced my mom's milk.

Border patrol can be extremely noisy. All the adults play a part in defending the territory of our pack. At dawn, noon, and sunset, we take turns guarding the borders and howl if we see any danger. There is often tension between packs. Smaller packs run away from larger packs, so the more of us there are, the better!

This is a typical target.
Poor little grass rat… he won't last long. Small rodents like this make up most of my diet. I'm cunning because I try to hunt when rodents are above ground. It gives me more chances to catch one. If there aren't many rodents around, I dig them out of their burrows.

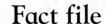

When I'm on the prowl, I keep a low profile.
This is what I do when I spot a rodent to eat. I lower my body close to the ground, flatten my tail, and creep up slowly and quietly. Once I'm near my prey, I run in and grab it tightly between my jaws.

Fact file

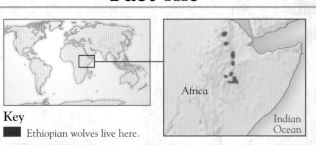

Africa

Indian Ocean

Key
Ethiopian wolves live here.

Population
= 200

The number of Ethiopian wolves has fallen by about half in nineteen years.

| 1984 | | fewer than 1,000 |
| 2003 | | fewer than 500 |

Ethiopian wolves under threat
Hunting Some farmers believe Ethiopian wolves kill their sheep and have hunted them in revenge.

Habitat loss Some of the area is being converted into farmland.

Domestic dogs These dogs are used to protect herds of sheep from hyena attacks. However, dogs compete with wolves for food and pass on diseases.

I like to keep my head down.
As a pup, I slept in a den. Once I was full-grown, I joined the other adult wolves curled up on the mountains. I wrap my tail around me and tuck my nose under it to escape the cold.

Family safety is top priority.
Before I was born, Mom dug an underground home where I could live safely with my brothers and sisters. This was our den, and it was guarded by members of the pack. My mom still played with me and caught food for me when I was one year old.

 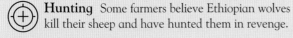

Mountain gorilla

I'm a gentle giant, so don't let my size scare you. Although I'm the largest living ape, I am rarely aggressive. I prefer life in the slow lane. I'm peaceful and relaxed, and I spend the day roaming the forest for food. I'm more like you than you realize. I smile, feel lots of emotions, and can even remember things that happened years ago.

I didn't stay small for long.
I developed quicker than you as a baby. At birth, we are all covered in black hair. Our mothers are very caring and give us constant attention. I snuggled up to my mom at night.

Here's my family enjoying a picnic.
We're digging in to some tasty, crumbly wood, which is a treat in the African mountains. We have strong family ties and often sit down to eat together, as well as play and groom each other.

Did you know?

We catch diseases. The most common one is pneumonia, which we might catch during the cold, wet season.

The first recorded sighting of one of us was by a German army officer in 1902, but the Africans who live near us knew we were there before that—they just didn't write it down.

The temperature here regularly drops to below freezing at night.

We rarely attack people. If you meet us, stay still and don't stare!

Look how scary we can be!
Adult males like me are much heavier than females, so we can defend our families. If my family is threatened, I bare my teeth and beat my chest, but if they are under attack, I use my terrifying strength to protect them. I'm fearless because my family comes first.

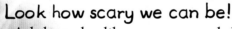

We munch the day away.
As vegetarians, our menu includes berries, nettles, thistles, and leaves. We never eat all the plants, though. Instead, we leave enough to continue growing for the next time we pass this way.

  Learn about gorillas by visiting the Dian Fossey Gorilla Fund International at www.gorillafund.org

Fact file

Key
 Mountain gorillas live here.

Africa • Indian Ocean

Population
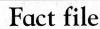 = 300

1989 fewer than 630
2003 fewer than 710

The populations of other gorillas are falling rapidly. Mountain gorillas are the only gorilla showing a slight increase in numbers.

Mountain gorillas under threat

 Converting to farmland Mountain gorillas live in national parks. These parks are shrinking as land is used for farming.

Pet trade These gorillas are hunted because their babies are sold as pets.

 Disease As more people use the forest, they risk spreading human diseases to the mountain gorillas.

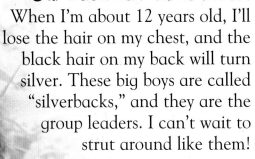

Our back hair turns silver.
When I'm about 12 years old, I'll lose the hair on my chest, and the black hair on my back will turn silver. These big boys are called "silverbacks," and they are the group leaders. I can't wait to strut around like them!

Mountain gorilla fur is particularly thick, shaggy, and long. It's ideal for the wet mountain climate because it protects them from chills.

I'm a smart guy.
I can recognize other gorillas by looking at their faces and body shapes. It's the same way that you can tell people apart. You might think that we all look the same, but we're quite different in appearance. Even the wrinkles over our noses are completely individual.

 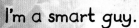

Snow leopard

Think of me as the invisible cat. You can't hear me because I can't roar. You can't see me because I live in some of the highest and most remote mountains in the world. Even if you climbed these peaks, you still wouldn't see me because my pale, furry coat merges with the landscape. I'm the least known of all the big cats, but I'm here to share my secrets.

I know where to find a bed. When I was a cub, I slept in a den. Now that I'm grown up, I'm less fussy. Craggy rocks and cliff ledges are comfy enough. They give me a good lookout point for prey, as well as possible danger.

Did you know?

We are excellent jumpers. We've been known to jump the length of two buses—about double the length any person has ever jumped.

Some of us live on Mount Everest, the world's highest mountain.

My front legs are shorter than my back legs and this helps me to climb up and over steep rocks.

Other big cats might eat you for breakfast, but there is no record of a snow leopard ever killing a human.

• The snow leopard's nose is large on the inside. As cold air is breathed in, it is warmed in the nose before going down to the lungs.

I love playing in the snow.
Snow can fall all year, but living in this climate is easier than you might think. I can cope with the cold. My large, puffy paws stop me from sinking into the snow, and I'm covered in long, woolly fur to keep warm.

🖑 Find out more by visiting the International Snow Leopard Trust at www.snowleopard.org

Can you tell I'm hungry?

At dawn and dusk, I hide out in crevices like this and keep watch for prey. When I see a possible meal below me, I go for it. I have to, because I don't know when the next opportunity to eat will come.

I have a multipurpose tail!

My furry tail is so big it's almost half my total length. It helps me balance on these uneven slopes, especially if I'm running over rocks. At night, it doubles up as a blanket to wrap around me.

I can kill prey three times bigger than me.

Just look at this ibex! I catch and kill a goat or sheep of this size about every two weeks. The rest of the time, rodents and birds make up my menu.

Fact file

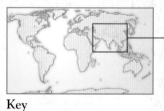

Asia

Key
■ Snow leopards live here.

Indian Ocean

Population

Numbers are difficult to record because the snow leopard is hard to spot. Footprints in the snow and signs like urine and scratch marks are used to help estimate figures.

	= 2,000

2003 | 🐆🐆🐆🐆 fewer than 7,500

Cubs learn a survival program.

Females have cubs in spring. This is the same time that sheep and goats are born. They're our main food supply. My mom and I stayed together for two years while she showed me how to fend for myself.

Snow leopards under threat

 Hunting Although the snow leopard is protected by law, local hunting continues. The fur is used to make clothing, and the bones are used in traditional medicine.

 Increased human population Because more people are now living in the area, snow leopards are forced to live even higher up the mountains.

Spectacled bear

I look like I'm wearing glasses. I'm not, of course. My name comes from the fact that I have light-colored fur around my eyes. I'd certainly never need glasses because my eyesight is fine. I also have a strong sense of smell, and I quickly sniff out sweet things. My senses come in very handy in the forests of the Andes Mountains. I'm special because I'm South America's only bear.

Sparks can fly when bear meets bear.
Although I'm usually quiet and shy, I can get aggressive if I meet another bear. If a neighbor gets too close, there's sure to be a lot of noise, and a fight might break out. We're much happier when we're left to ourselves!

The eye markings of the spectacled bear are one way to tell the different bears apart. Each bear has its own individual pattern of creamy fur.

Did you know?

We feature regularly in the folklore, religion, and legends of many of the different groups of people from the Andes.

We spread fruit seeds around the mountains. Seeds left in our droppings grow into new fruit trees.

Except for the mountain tapir, we are the largest land mammal in South America.

As with all bears, our fathers play no part in helping to raise us.

This looks yummy.
Most of the time, we eat a vegetarian diet. Fruit, leaves, grasses, bulbs, and bromeliad plants like this one are our foods of choice. Another favorite is the fruit of a cactus, but we watch out for the prickles.

I couldn't do without my strong jaw muscles.
This bromeliad is a tough, tropical plant, but I can bite through it with ease and grind it up with my teeth. I usually rip out plants from the ground. If I see some tempting fruit high up in a tree, though, I'll make the extra effort to climb up and get it.

To find out about the spectacled bear sanctuary, visit Bear Rescue at www.bear-rescue.tv

I'm good at swimming.

Here I am enjoying the water. As usual, I'm on my own. We're solitary bears, except for mothers with cubs. The only time you see us gather together is when there is an area with plenty of fruit trees. Even though we eat together, we ignore each other.

Fact file

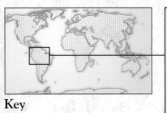

South America

Pacific Ocean

Key

■ Spectacled bears live here.

Population

 = 500

2003 |  2,000

This figure is only an estimate. Since these bears are shy animals who sleep during the day, not much is known about them and little research has been carried out.

Spectacled bears under threat

 Habitat loss The area where the spectacled bears live is being destroyed. The forests are being cut down and the land is being turned into farmland.

Hunting These bears are hunted for sport, as well as their fur and meat. Farmers have also killed spectacled bears because they raid crop fields.

I own my own tree house.

I can climb trees easily with my sharp claws, so I often make myself a platform up here where I can eat and rest. It's a nest of branches, which I cover with layers of leaves. It's really quite comfy! I like to sit down and eat the fruit I've picked from nearby trees.

We're born in time for the best food supply.

Cubs are born when fruit ripens. At this time, mothers eat a lot of fruit. This diet ensures that they produce the milk they need to feed their cubs. Mothers and cubs live in dens, which are often tree hollows. When I was small, Mom carried me on her back as we searched for food. I stayed with her for two years.

Apollo butterfly

You'll find me gliding on the wind at high altitudes in Europe and central Asia. Here, I feed on nectar-rich flowers, such as thistles. The bright red and orange spots on my wings look like the eyes of a larger animal and stop me from being attacked by birds. My baby caterpillars have spots similar to mine.

 Habitat destruction threatens the Apollo butterfly.

Mountain watch

Many mammals in this habitat have thick fur to prevent them from losing heat in the cold temperatures. The takin is one example. Because the ground is often uneven and dangerous, some animals have strong, small feet to help them leap safely around the rock ledges. Others, such as the red panda, have long tails to help them balance in the trees and on the slopes.

Long-beaked echidna

Would you eat worms for dinner? They are my main source of food up here in the mountains on the island of New Guinea. I use my long snout to sniff them out, and then I hook them on my spiked tongue. My body is also covered in spikes. If I sense danger, I dig down, leaving only my sharp spines above the surface.

 Hunting is the main threat, since people eat the meat of long-beaked echidnas.

Takin

Look at my gorgeous golden fur. It has been said that the legendary golden fleece sought by Jason and the Argonauts was inspired by my coat. I'm a stocky goat antelope living in the Himalayas and western China. Most of the time, I eat leaves and grass, but I also get through a lot of salt from mineral deposits near here.

 Habitat loss is thought to be the biggest threat to the takin.

The development of ski resorts has left these frogs with a much smaller area to live in.

Southern corroboree frog

I'm a funky-looking frog from Australia. My bold stripes are the same colors as a bumblebee's. While the back of me feels hard and rough, my tummy feels soft and smooth. If I think that predators might be nearby, my skin can produce a natural poison to protect me. We live in groups, and talk to each other by making squelching sounds.

The mountain forests where red pandas live are being cleared for farming.

Red panda

When I'm on the ground, I lumber around slowly and awkwardly, but as soon as I get up in the trees, I turn into a skilled climber. I live in the forests of the Himalayas and parts of China and Myanmar. Between dawn and dusk, you'll see me roaming around looking for bamboo to eat. I might take a break around noon and spend the night snoozing in a tree.

Andean people have collected many flamingo eggs to eat.

Andean flamingo

We are the picture of elegance, with our graceful, curved beaks and long, long legs. We like the peaceful solitude of lakes and lagoons in the mountains of South America. This is where we dip our big beaks into the shallow waters to feed on our tiny food, called algae. If we're lucky, we can live about 50 years.

How you can help

Here are some of the organizations working to save the world's endangered animals.

Whether you want to learn more about the animals featured in this book, find out about world habitats, or even adopt one of the animals, these websites provide in-depth information and show you how to get involved.

 Forest

www.arkive.org/wolverine
Take a look at the scary wolverine in the snow of North America.

www.arkive.org/philippine-eagle
Find out more about this huge eagle and see it in flight.

www.arkive.org/golden-frog
It'll be hard to miss this brightly colored frog.

www.arkive.org/mandrill
See inside the huge mouth of the mandrill as it yawns.

www.arkive.org/pygmy-hippopotamus
Watch a video of the pygmy hippopotamus going for a dip in the river and swimming underwater.

www.arkive.org/asiatic-lion
See footage of an Asiatic lion grooming her cub, as well as a cub yawning and stretching.

www.janegoodall.org
This institute was founded by Jane Goodall, the well-known chimpanzee researcher. The institute aims to encourage the conservation of chimpanzees and other primates.

 Desert

www.arkive.org/coral-pink-sand-dunes-tiger-beetle
Film footage shows this beetle burrowing into the sand and disappearing from sight.

www.arkive.org/woma-python
Watch a woma python winding its way across the sand dunes.

www.arkive.org/northern-hairy-nosed-wombat
See how big and cuddly this wombat is.

www.arkive.org/desert-tortoise
Observe these tortoises feeding on colorful desert flowers.

www.arkive.org/saiga-antelope
See saiga antelopes caught in snowstorms at their winter feeding grounds.

www.arkive.org/greater-bilby
Take a look at newborn bilbies inside their mother's pouch.

www.desertusa.com/animal.html
Discover how animals in the desert have adapted to this harsh habitat, and meet many of the desert dwellers.

www.livingdesert.org
This website looks at desert animals around the world.

 Ocean

www.arkive.org/great-white-shark
Take a look at film footage of a great white shark leaping out of the water to catch its prey.

www.arkive.org/hectors-dolphin
See a group of dolphins swimming along and hear the noises they make!

www.arkive.org/wandering-albatross
Watch footage of a wandering albatross flying over stormy seas, and landing on a snowy hillside.

www.arkive.org/manta-ray
Watch a manta ray swimming through the ocean.

www.arkive.org/leafy-seadragon
Learn how a seadragon catches its prey.

www.arkive.org/whale-shark
View a whale shark feeding, and see its tiny teeth up close.

Animal adoption

www.sandiegozoo.org/society/adoption.html
You can adopt one of many mammals, birds, and reptiles at the San Diego Zoo.

wcs.org/getinvolved/adoption-center
Sponsor a jaguar or a tiger and help conserve wildlife around the world.

www.torontozoo.com
The Toronto Zoo is home to 5,000 animals and there are a variety available for adoption.

www.pandasinternational.org
If you've got a preference for pandas, this is the website for you.

How you can help

Exploring habitats

www.mountainnature.com
Find out more about the mountain habitat and the wildlife living there.

www.seashepherd.org
This conservation society is working to conserve and restore the oceans.

www.oceanconservancy.org
The Ocean Conservancy is striving to improve the oceans.

www.antarctica.ac.uk
The British Antarctic Survey is responsible for research in Antarctica.

www.rainforest.org.uk
This organization protects forests and animals under threat.

www.rainforest-alliance.org
Rainforest Alliance supports the conservation of rainforests.

Grassland

www.arkive.org/mexican-prairie-dog
Find out more about the prairie dogs who stand guard over their burrows.

www.arkive.org/great-indian-bustard
See the great Indian bustard in flight.

www.arkive.org/rufous-hare-wallaby
Take a look at the wallaby feeding during the night.

www.arkive.org/african-wild-dog
Watch footage of an African wild dog digging out a den.

www.arkive.org/takahe
Here you can see a takahe splashing around in water as it takes a bath.

www.arkive.org/black-footed-ferret
See a litter of newborn ferrets.

www.savetherhino.org
Save the Rhino is committed to saving rhinoceroses by supporting projects that protect them and by raising awareness.

http://lynx.uio.no/catfolk/
This website includes news and research about all the big cats.

Mountain

www.arkive.org/apollo-butterfly
See the Apollo butterfly on rocks, leaves, and lavender.

www.arkive.org/long-beaked-echidna
Watch a long-beaked echidna feeding.

www.arkive.org/takin
Get a glimpse of the takin walking around its natural habitat.

www.arkive.org/red-panda
Here you can see the red panda taking a nap up in a tree.

www.arkive.org/southern-corroboree-frog
See this frog at home in its habitat and even hear it croaking.

www.arkive.org/andean-flamingo
Observe Andean flamingoes preening, feeding, and flying.

www.mountaingorillas.org
The International Gorilla Conservation Program (IGCP) wants to protect mountain gorillas and their habitat.

www.raysweb.net/wildlife
This website contains great photographs of the varied wildlife found in the Rocky Mountains.

Other organizations

www.worldwildlife.org
This is the website of the World Wildlife Fund, the largest international conservation organization in the world.

www.careforthewild.org/kids.asp
A wildlife charity set up to protect animals from exploitation.

www.earthwatch.org
Earthwatch is an international organization that cares for the planet by organizing expeditions to remote, threatened areas.

www.foe.co.uk
Friends of the Earth is a well-known international network of environmental groups.

www.defenders.org
Defenders of Wildlife is dedicated to protecting wild animals.

www.rspb.org.uk/youth
The Royal Society for the Protection of Birds is Europe's largest conservation charity.

www.wdcs.org
A charity that campaigns for the protection of whales, dolphins, and porpoises around the world.

www.unep-wcmc.org
The World Conservation Monitoring Center keeps a record of which animals are endangered.

www.durrellwildlife.org
Durrell Wildlife's mission is to save wild animals from extinction.

www.wildaid.org
This organization is helping to stop the illegal wildlife trade.

Index

A,B

albatross, wandering 48
anteater, giant 60–61
antelope, Saiga 35
ass, Indian wild 32–33
bear, spectacled 74–75
bilby, greater 34
boat traffic 37, 45
breeding 13, 57
bustard, great Indian 62
butterfly, Apollo 76

C,D

camel, wild Bactrian 26–27
camouflage 18, 29, 31, 48, 58, 61, 72
cheetah 52–53
deforestation 9, 11, 15, 17, 67
desert 22–23
dog, African wild 63
dolphin, Hector's 49
drinking 10, 22, 25, 26, 27, 29, 31, 32, 33, 35, 58, 61
drought 29, 33

E,F

eagle, Philippine 20
echidna, long-beaked 76
elephant, African 24–25
farming 51, 55, 65, 71

ferret, black-footed 63
fires 9, 11, 15, 51, 61
fishing nets 37, 39, 41
flamingo, Andean 77
food shortage 19, 23, 53
forest 8–9
frog, golden 20
    Southern corroboree 77

G,H

Gila monster 30–31
gorilla, mountain 70–71
grassland 50–51
habitat loss 19, 27, 31, 33, 57, 59, 61, 69, 75
habitats: desert 22–23
    forest 8–9
    grassland 50–51
    mountain 64–65
    ocean 36–37
hippo, pygmy 21
human population 17, 23, 25, 65, 67, 71, 73
hunting 13, 15, 19, 25, 27, 29, 33, 39, 41, 43, 45, 47, 55, 59, 67, 69, 73, 75

I,J,K

iguana, marine 42–43
kakapo 12–13
koala 16–17

L,M

leopard, snow 72–73
lion, Asiatic 21
macaw, hyacinth 56–57
manatee, West Indian 44–45
mandrill 21
mountain 64–65

N,O

ocean 36–37
orangutan 10–11
oryx, Arabian 28–29

P,Q

panda, giant 66–67
    red 77
pet trade 11, 31, 57, 71
pollution 37, 39, 41, 43, 45
prairie dog, Mexican 62–63
python, Woma 34

R,S

ray, manta 49
rhinoceros, black 54–55
sea cow 44–45
seadragon, leafy 48
sea otter 40–41
shark, great white 48
    whale 49

sifaka, Verreaux's 14–15
sleeping 10, 17, 21, 31, 32, 34, 41, 42, 45, 60, 66, 67, 69, 72, 77, 79
swimming 19, 21, 27, 38, 40, 41, 43, 44, 45, 46, 47, 48, 49, 61, 66, 75, 78

T,U

takahe 63
takin 76
tiger 18–19
tiger beetle 34
tortoise, desert 35
tourism 37, 45, 47, 65
traps 20, 21, 53
turtle, green 46–47

V,W

wallaby, rufous hare 62
whale, humpback 38–39
wolf, Ethiopian 68–69
wolverine 20
wombat, hairy-nosed 35

X,Y,Z

zebra, Grevy's 58–59

Acknowledgments and Credits

Dorling Kindersley would like to thank :

Sheila Collins; ARKive researchers Verity Greenwood BSc, PhD and Michelle Lindley BSc, MSc

The publisher would like to thank the following for their kind permission to reproduce their photographs :

(Key: a-above; c-center; b-below; l-left; r-right; t-top)
Alamy Images: Andy Rouse 72tc; Aqua Image 47tr; Barrie Harwood LRPS LBPPA 3br; ImageState/Mike Hill 73tl; Joe Thraves 59br; Martin Harvey 69cr; Paul Brough 28tl; Pete Oxford/Steve Bloom Images 5bc; Stephen Frink Collection/James D Watt 47cr; Steve Bloom Images 25clb, 66c, 67br, 73br; Wildphotos.com 33cb; Wolfgang Polzer 43tl. Ardea.com: Adrian Warren 66cr; Alan Greensmith 13cla, 62tl; Bill Coster 37cl; D. Parer & E. Parer-Cook 58tl; Francois Gohier 31tc, 38br, 40cl; Ian Beames 74tl; Joanna Van Gruisen 62b; John Cancalosi 63bl; John Daniels 1, 65c, 72cr; M. Watson 21tr, 75tl, 77t; Mary Clay 31clb; Masahiro Iijima 20tr. Auscape: Ben Cropp 5cb; David Parer & Elizabeth Parer-Cook 76cr; Doug Perrine 37cr; Erwin & Peggy Bauer 22cr; Francois Gohier 39tr; Frank Woerle 34cr; Jean-Paul Ferrero 77tr; John Shaw 16c; Yves Arthus-Bertrand 71cr. Christine Breton: 34tl. Bruce Coleman Inc: John H. Hoffman 60tr, 60c. Phillip Colla/OceanLight.com: 38cb, 39br, 45clb. Corbis: 5c, 57c, Amos Nachoum 38tl; Anthony Bannister; Gallo Images 24bl; Buddy Mays 55bl; D. Robert & Lorri Franz 63br, 72b; Douglas Faulkner 44c; Gallo Images 14cr, 15cb, 68clb, 69cal; George D. Lepp 11crb; Jeffrey L. Rotman 43tr; Joe McDonald 51c, 55tl, 55c, 59tl;

Karl Ammann 2-3b, 58br; Kennan Ward 35t, 40b; Kevin Schafer 74b; Martin Harvey 64cr; Martin Harvey/Gallo Images 9c, 10br, 14bc, 15l, 54tl; Michael & Patricia Fogden 34b; Nigel J. Dennis, Gallo Images 25ca; Ron Sanford 38tr; Sanford/Agliolo 41t; Steve Kaufman 28cra; Stuart Westmorland 47bl; Theo Allofs 2t; Tom Brakefield 9cr, 11br, 60-61b; Wolfgang Kaehler 11ca, 43bl; Yogi, Inc 23cl. Don Merton: Crown Copyright: Department of Conservation Te Papa Atawhai 2004: 12tr, 13c, 13tr; Crown Copyright. Department of Conservation, New Zealand. 2004 12bl. Foto Natura: Martin Harvey 53br. FLPA - images of nature: Foto Natura Stock 61cla; Frans Lanting/Minden Pictures 51cr, 55cl; Fred Bavendam/Minden Pictures 40clb; Fritz Polking 57br; Gerard Lacz 14l, 41br; Minden Pictures/Gerry Ellis 70tr; Mitsuaki Iwago/Minden Pictures 16bl; Shin Yoshino/Minden Pictures 17c; Tui de Roy/Minden Pictures 6-7. Getty Images: Aldo Brando 42tr; Anup Shah 19b; Art Wolfe 26-27b, 42b; Darrell Gulin 59cl; David Noton 4tc, 8-9; James Balog 66cl; Jeff Hunter 46-47c; Joseph Van Os 18t, 54bl; Keren Su 64c; Paul Souders 53ca; Pete Turner 17tl; Photographer's Choice 46b; Renee Lynn 10-11c; Steve Bloom 53t; Tim Flach 31b. Lonely Planet Images: ABI 4cb, 50-51; Casey & Astrid Witte Mahaney 4c, 36-37; John Hay 18b; Mark Newman 4bc, 64-65. N.H.P.A.: Andy Rouse 3tc; Ant Photo Library 16cl, 36c, 49t; Daniel Heuclin 30bl; Haroldo Palo Jr 56bc; Joe Blossom 18cra; Kevin Schafer 57bl; Martin Harvey 19tr, 51cl, 62tr, 69tr, 70c, 70-71b; Nick Garbutt 20bl; Nigel J Dennis 25br; Rich Kirchner 73tr. Natural Visions: Heather Angel 26bcl. Nature Picture Library Ltd: Aflo 36cr; Anup Shah 10tr, 10bl, 19cl, 23cr, 32bl, 33br, 33t; Ashok Jain 21b; Brandon Cole 47cb; Brent Hedges 48bl; Bruce Davidson 63tr; Charlie Hamilton James 68tr, 69b; Dave Watts 35clb;

Doug Allan 48-49c; Francois Savigny 4bl, 74c, 75c; Gertrud & Helmut Denzau 5ca, 27cl, 32cl, 32br, 33cr; Hanne & Jens Eriksen 28c, 28-29tc, 29cl; Jeff Foott 44bl; Jeff Rotman 49b; Jim Clarke 75clb; Jurgen Freund 46tr; Lynn M. Stone 67tl; Nick Garbutt 9cl; Paul Johnson 35br; Pete Oxford 15br, 65cr, 76bl, 77b; Peter Scoones 48tl; Philippe Clement 76tl; Sharon Heald 24c; Staffan Widstrand 50cr, 56-57c; Todd Pusser 49cr; Tony Heald 24cl, 25tr, 59tr. National Geographic Image Collection: Brian J. Skerry 45t; Chris Johns 50c; James L Stanfield 26l; Jason Edwards 42tl; Tim Laman 8c, 65cl. photolibrary.com/Oxford Scientific Films: Alan Root 61br; Andrew Plumptre 70bl, 71tr; Brian Kenney 27t; Owen Newman 68r; Colin Monteath 27br; Javed Jafferji 46cra; John Harris/SAL 31cla; Konrad Wothe 56cl; Lon E Lauber 41c; Mike Hill 28b; Robin Bush 8cr, 13b; Stan Ossolinski 58cl; Steffen Hauser 74clb. Powerstock: Age Fotostock/Peter Liilja 20c; Georgie Holland 46br; Michael S. Nolan 38-39c; Morales 22c. Ian Redmond: 70bc. Science Photo Library: Ted Clutter 60cl, 61tl. Dr Mark Seward: 30c. Still Pictures: Alpha Presse/Carlo Dani & Ingrid Jeske 19cr; Bios/Martin Harvey 14tr; Fred Bavendam 44tr, 45b; Martin Harvey 53cra; Michael Sewell 40tr; Peter Arnold 73c; Pu Tao 67cl; Robert Henno 37c; X. Eichaker 29r. Dick Veitch: Crown Copyright: Department of Conservation Te Papa Atawhai 2004 12r. Visuals Unlimited Inc: Jim Merli 30tr; Mary McDonald 23c; Theo Allofs 17bc. James Warwick: 57tl. Dave Watts: 21tl. Woodfall Wild Images: Ted Mead 4ca, 22-23. World Wildlife Fund: David Lawson 52t. Robert J Young: 61tr. Zefa Visual Media: Daryl Benson 5t; Jeremy Woodhouse 43cr; W. Wisniewski 52b.
All other images © Dorling Kindersley www.dkimages.com